UNDERSTANDING YOUR **FINANCES** THROUGH LIFE'S **CHANGES:**

CLOSING THE RELATIONSHIP GAP IN FINANCIAL LITERACY

Special Thanks to:

My wife Vanessa Marie Perez Etienne and my daughter
Delaney E. Etienne

Joseph & Melida Etienne

Evena, Berl-Yves, Marthen, Caelle, Cailan, and Nathen Mercier

Lourdes Ductan

Ernest London

Jose Y. Etienne

Daisy Sylvestre

"This material is not intended to replace the advice of a qualified tax advisor, attorney, accountant or financial advisor"

For more resources please go to www.madbu.com and madbumax.com

Contents

INTRODUCTION

Managing personal finances can be very challenging to some people. Overcoming obstacles that can affect your personal and family's financial path is a goal that requires planning, commitment, and strategy. Financial education plays an important role in financial management because managing numbers and finances is a big challenge for many because people tend not to like dealing with numbers.

Some people do not even address their finances because of their inability to organize and plan a personal budget, thus making it a difficult task to believe that they can get on top of their finances. If you don't know how to manage your finances, to some people, the solution is to make the world's best spreadsheets or buy the best software; but it's not all! Success depends on the right behavior and the right tools. Some people just know when they get paid they will spend money until they get paid again. In these cases, some tools will help, but a change in mindset and behaviors should be the first thing to address.

This book highlights the need for financial responsibility. The book emphasizes that financial discretion as singles is financial security for the future. It's then followed with a discussion on budgets as a means to financial prudence, stating that having a budget is not necessarily about limited spending but flexibility in spending. In the second part, the discussion continues with openness and sincerity about your financial position and talking it over with your partner. Finally, in the third part of this book, the author discusses budgeting for your wedding and honeymoon, and how to avoid unnecessary expenses while planning for your wedding. This book also has additional information about how to save money through the use of coupons, and how to earn addition income to supplement your financial freedom and retirement planning.

Part 1
FINANCIAL PLANNING WHILE SINGLE

A world's view

Financial planning is one of the processes of determining different approaches to earn, save, invest and spend money. By planning personal finances, one can manage the funds in a way that allows them to achieve their goals.[1] Personal finances refer to the financial management of an individual's resources. They comprise of how an individual manages their money through investments, savings and expenditures considering different risks and life events. Having different personal finance management strategies for different stages of life is very essential and allows one to simplify the task of investing for each stage.

Single

When single, many people think that they have very few expenses and also fewer resources to warrant a financial plan, given that most people are starting their lives. When one is single, saving and investing can seem like an unnecessary and impossible task as many people may see their paychecks as an easier way to get through each month and not planning for the future.[2]

However, it is important to note that it is at this stage when one can easily establish their financial base for the rest of their lives. At this stage, personal finances are important in that one can plan themselves for career training and also plan on how to pay

---

[1] Melin Emilsson, Ulla, and Agneta Ståhl. "Good personal finances or a strong social capital—on different life conditions of importance for an active life when becoming alone in old age." *European Journal of Social Work* 19, no. 5 (2016): 749–763.

[2] Melin Emilsson, Ulla, and Agneta Ståhl (2016).

and manage student loans.[3] Therefore, managing one's finances helps a single person meet both their short term and long term goals without having to go beyond the income limits.

Understanding personal finances at this time also give one ample time to start budgeting and saving for the future and avoid overspending on status symbols such as expensive cars. Understanding personal finances can, therefore, help one to prioritize where money should go, which is done by determining the most significant goals and how to get to them. At this stage, disregarding knowledge about personal finances could result in an individual unintentionally squandering some of their biggest assets in their lives as they think they don't have much responsibility.[4] With power of understanding personal finances, a single person can save or invest, which can then grow exponentially but when one thinks of waiting until they are married, they might need to contribute more to have similar results.

Understanding personal finance also keeps one off unmanageable debts which can be dangerous on one's future finances. One is able to take responsibility for their financial future and despite the many things that may be out of control for young and single adults, they need to keep their finances on track. Other importance of understanding personal finances and having financial goals is that the single adults become financially independent at an early age, develop a savings plan

---

[3] Zimbardo, Philip, Nick Clements, and Umbelina Rego Leite. "Time perspective and financial health: to improve financial health, traditional financial literacy skills are not sufficient. understanding your time perspective is critical." In *Time Perspective*, pp. 9–40. Palgrave Macmillan, London, 2017.

[4] Banthia, Dhananjay, and Sujata Mangaraj. "ALiterature Review on Financial Literacy-APathway for Achieving Financial Freedom." *Siddhant-A Journal of Decision Making* 17, no. 1 (2017): 98-102.

and also can carefully manage the use of credit. The bottom line is that the earlier one starts saving and investing, the more time they have to grow and there is no better time to establish good money habits than when one is single.

CHAPTER ONE
FINANCIAL SECURITY FOR THE FUTURE

There is a lot of help and information available for family finance, but what about singles, either by choice or circumstances? Organizing finances is not a simple task. But, in general, it can be considered easier when you are still single. After all, having a married life or starting a family generates a series of extra expenses to include in the budget. So, if financial organization has been a challenge in your life, it is important to find a way to overcome this challenge, as it will be easier to organize your routine and take advantage of this phase to save money and ensure a more comfortable future while you are still single.

The first step in exercising greater financial control is to know your budget. Whether it's a parent's allowance, internship scholarship, freelance work, or a formal job salary, you need to put all your income and expenses on paper. A financial control application is very useful at this point. It allows you to easily record everything that comes in and out of your account. Thus, it is easy to monitor your financial movements and know what your budget is like. However, it is not enough to record your income and expenses. It is also necessary to assess your consumption pattern and make some financial planning. That is, you must, in fact, be in control of your budget.

To do this, try dividing your spending by categories and analyzing the graphs that the finance application offers. They promote very efficient assessments of your financial life. That way, you will know exactly how much you have spent in each category, such as transportation, food, housing, etc. From there, it is possible to put a spending cap and decide more consciously how to use your money. Another very interesting utility of the finance application is to control the maturity dates of your accounts: you record and track payments, preventing arrears and charging interest. Financial planning for singles also needs to involve the economy. To do this, it is essential to control your consumption and avoid unnecessary expenses or impulse purchases. This is one of the biggest challenges of financial control, especially when we consider that single life usually involves significant spending on leisure. The lower demand with fixed accounts allows for greater freedom. However, this should not mean financial uncontrolled.

To find out if you're spending money on unnecessary things, assess your costs over the past few months and see if there's anything that could have been cut. Also note possible underutilized services in your routines, such as cable TV or internet package and telephone. The ideal is not to cut everything that is considered superfluous. After all, it is important to have the autonomy to spend money on things that make you happy. The point is to save on what is not so important and thus have more money for your priorities. In the task of controlling your purchases, moderation in the use of credit cards is essential. The young bachelor is at greater risk of losing control of credit and ending up with large debts. So, don't forget that small monthly expenses accumulate and can end up with a big bill. Ideally, you should record credit card expenditures in your finance application as soon as they are made. That way, you can monitor how you use them throughout the month.

Another essential precaution is not to consider the card limit as an extra income. In reality, it is one more account. That is, don't use it as an income supplement when the money runs out at the end of the month. Each expense on the card must be planned, like all the others you make. Taking advantage of promotional periods in stores is one of the most efficient ways to save. Supermarket expenses, for example, can decrease a lot if you develop the habit of following the discount campaigns carried out by companies. The same idea goes for other purchases. On the internet, it is possible to compare prices in different places, find promotions and discount coupons, and even buy products for much lower prices. Even large expenses can be greatly reduced by looking for promotions. This is the case with travel - on websites of accommodation or group purchases, you find very competitive prices. Look for the same tour on different websites.

One of the main villains of financial planning for singles is leisure. After all, this is usually a phase that involves many outings with friends, trips, concerts, and other entertainment programs. At the end of the month, it doesn't come cheap. But, of course, nobody wants to put aside their happiness and quality of life just to save money. So, what's the way out? The best option is to look for cheaper alternatives to maintain your social life and replace some of your programs. For example, a party night can be exchanged for having friends at home for less money. A similar idea can be used to replace going to the cinema with a film at home. It is important to highlight that we are not talking about doing this with all the outings of the month - only with some.

A very interesting possibility is to find out what entertainment options your city offers. In capital cities, mainly tourist ones, it is common to have free events (such as exhibitions and shows). In addition, you can enjoy squares, parks, and other spaces to have fun with friends. If you want to be truly successful in your financial planning, it is important to know the concept of the emergency reserve. It is essential to maintain a balanced budget and offer security even in times of financial crisis.

Think about what you would do today if you run out of income. It would probably be necessary to stop your consumption and adapt your routine to a reality without income, right? The purpose of the emergency reserve is precisely to avoid this. That is, this reserve is money that you save and make available for emergency moments. It can be used to pay for unforeseen expenses, resolve emergencies, and offer financial balance when you experience instability.

With these ideas, you have everything you need to set up incredible financial planning for singles. That way, you will be able to have a more balanced life and do more with your money, without forgetting to prepare for the future.

WHAT DOES IT MEAN TO BE SINGLE?

The fact is that being single can be easier to manage than being married. This starts with the use of the remote control! Marriage can be tiring to some. After all, when you are part of a couple, you have your relationship with your friends and family, the relationship of your partner with friends and family, and the relationship of the couple itself. When you're single, there aren't three relationships to manage, only ONE. Look how beautiful that is! Only your relationship with the world: friends, family, and co-workers.

From a financial point of view, there are several advantages to being married: the couple's joint income can offer greater security against unforeseen circumstances. It is also possible to divide the expenses in the case of more expensive investments, such as the purchase of a property. But would there be any financial advantage in remaining single? Yes, of course, there is! Many married couples should already know this answer, as they feel the additional expenses "in the skin" (and in the pocket). But it may be that "the plug has not yet fallen" for some singles ... so, let's go to the advantages!

The life of a couple requires certain joint agreements and commitments; after all, the opinions and objectives (future or immediate) of the two do not always converge. For example, one may be looking to save a lot to buy a home while the other prioritizes taking trips and seeing the world. In order to reach a consensus on what the couple's financial planning will be, a lot of conversation and "negotiation" will be necessary. This whole process is important and healthy, but it will also consume everyone's time. Singles have the great privilege to decide for themselves! They may even seek different opinions, but the whole process is much faster.

Traveling in a group or accompanied is usually much better than traveling alone. The problem with the couple's trip is the need to "synchronize the schedules," as both have to take a vacation at the same time. And we will not even comment here on the scenario with children because then the trip can only happen during school holidays; that is, in the high season. This restriction can make tickets and hotels more expensive. So, enjoy it while you have the chance to decide to travel overnight, on a Tuesday afternoon, after getting a break from work!

In the same way that your partner can help with household accounts, he or she can also make the situation much worse! If one of the two goes into debt, most likely, the most financially balanced partner will have to help the least balanced with their finances.

It's amazing how singles can survive on a simple, inexpensive diet! You don't need anything elaborate, you can even eat the same type of food for days in a row, and it won't be the end of the world (at least for most people). That seems to change with marriage. The meal, especially dinner, becomes a more social and important moment, demanding a certain quality in the meal! And that will generate more expenses ... but at least you will eat better!

It is important to be financially prudent while you are single. This will help with building a healthy relationship. In order to achieve this comfortably, there are six steps that need to be put in place now that you have the total freedom to do so.

- Get every financial statement you can

- Record all of your income sources

- Create a list of monthly expenses

- Split expenses into two categories: fixed and variable

- Sum your monthly income and expenses

- Make adjustments to expenses

1. GET EVERY FINANCIAL STATEMENT YOU CAN

Control your cash flow, design scenarios, develop action plans. You should already be fully aware that planning makes all the difference in your life and how you get to live it, and that this occurs in all areas: strategy, management, operations, etc. It is through planning that you think critically about your income and expenses, define objectives, design scenarios, and define action plans. Financial planning is an essential part of this process, which could be achieved with your previous and current financial pieces of information.

It is good to know a financial projection statement serves to project your income and expenses, with the purpose of indicating the economic situation and how you should live to manage it. By doing so, you can clearly see how much you intend to bill, spend, invest, and profit; thus, you're able to plan the best way to use your resources. The financial statement is more than important; it is indispensable. Because, at the bottom, it is the basis for almost all of your practices. Without doing it correctly, you will not be able to make strategic decisions for yourself and save. If you have not evaluated your projections, you will find yourself unable to analyze and apply your investments at the right time, review costs, and identify the best opportunities to optimize your activities. Still, as important as it is, the number of singles who ignore this aspect is unbelievable. As a result, it is not surprising that the number of people who regret their time spent when they are single.

A good financial statement is not feasible if you do not know your current income level and how you plan to let it grow. Try to make a balance sheet – that is, an accounting statement that aims to present the financial and economic position considering your assets and liabilities. In knowing the exact situation, it is time to organize the financial planning spreadsheet. Start by writing down everything you intend to earn over a period; that is, plan your billing. The ideal would be to carry out financial plans for one-year, divided month by month. Build a sales plan reflecting your sources of revenue, your pricing model, your distribution channels, etc. Then, plan everything you will spend over a period. In addition to recurring expenses, be sure to include expenses that may be extraordinary or that will reflect new investments that you intend to make in order to achieve your goals. Then review the items and evaluate what is needed and what can be postponed. Build the financial statements that will give you a consolidated view of your financial situation for the year, the Income Statement, and the Balance Sheet. This way, you will be able to assess whether you are very aggressive at a certain time of the year, whether the projections seem realistic, whether you could optimize any spending, maximize your revenue, etc.

Unfortunately, the future remains unknown to all of us. However, anticipating different possibilities makes us better prepared for what comes – and that's what financial planning is also for. So, when it comes to putting your accounts on the tip of the pencil, don't hesitate to design different scenarios. Always try to work with three: an optimist, a realist, and a pessimist. After putting everything on paper, it's time to make action plans. It's time to roll up your sleeves and turn everything that has been recorded into reality.

2. RECORD ALL YOUR INCOME SOURCES

How much you earn determines how healthy you save. You need to keep track of what you earn and how you get to earn it. There are various methods of achieving this. You may have heard of passive income without knowing what it really is.

Passive income is one that will allow you to earn money without having to deal with it. Concretely, you will not have much to do or nothing to do to earn money. It may sound incredible, but some people actually make a living from this passive income. There are many solutions to generate passive income.

It's up to you to choose the passive income that will best meet your financial expectations. Be aware that work is still necessary beforehand to set up these sources of passive income. Nothing will just fall on your lap, and you will have to invest yourself at the start to be able to reap the rewards later. In the past, everyone put their money in a savings account and live off of the interest. Right now, things are very different. Interest rates are no longer attractive at all, and, therefore, it's not very interesting to save your hard-earned money only to see 0.75% to 1.50% each year, if you're lucky. By investing part of your savings in the market, you will be able to make your money grow by taking advantage of high returns, which generally approach 8% depending on the type of investment. Obviously, the risks are higher, but you can earn good profits. The risks lie, in particular, in the fact that you are going to lend money to companies or own part of these companies. It is, therefore, a good idea to invest your money in several different companies and not just one to help you have a wide source of income instead of making money idle over a period of time.

3. CREATE A LIST OF MONTHLY EXPENSES

Keeping good financial management practice could be much easier if there was no basic amenity. There is a need to create a preference for needs while making a list of wants. Managing money correctly is not a simple task. Many times, we fall into different temptations where unnecessary expenses can play tricks on us, or sometimes, we just don't have the money to save and have support in case of any need. However, with proper financial planning, you can create different strategies to best address the different scenarios and situations that arise in your life. Having a well-organized list of expenses helps to prevent the temptation of spending on unnecessary commodities.

4. SPLIT EXPENSES INTO TWO CATEGORIES

There is no fixed or predictable budget, so you need to plan your expenses every month. Life will change, time will change, the situation will change, and budgets will change. Experience has shown that this is as predictable as an increase in fixed costs and a decrease in variability. For example, monthly mortgages or rents, salaries paid as security, monthly repayments for a specific loan received, insurance and electricity, and water bills are part of the fixed costs. On the other hand, unpredictable or unexpected expenses, an expensive dinner from last night, shopping with friends, and receipts for expensive telephone plans are part of variable costs. There may be other types of variable costs, such as a sudden car breakdown, an immediate need to repair a house or office, or the need to buy a new phone.

What you can do in a month with a large number of planned or fixed costs is to plan the majority of expenses. You will then know what can help identify and reduce unnecessary costs. For example, you can access the cheap WiFi/phone plan and create a list of what you really need to buy. Also, periodically check your spending history over the past few months.

5. SUM YOUR MONTHLY INCOME AND EXPENSES

As for the budget, the only take-out is the income. Forget about profit before tax. You can use or save a single paycheck.

To check your monthly travel income:

<u>If you get paid fortnightly</u>

Multiply the salary by the takeaway salary by the number of annual salaries: 26. Simply divide the number by 12 to know the monthly income.

<u>If you get paid weekly</u>

You need to use the weekly wage and multiply by the number of weeks in a year: 52. Divide this number by 12 to get a monthly income.

<u>When salaries fluctuate</u>

Although your salary varies depending on tips, different hours, and/or commissions, you can still calculate your estimated monthly income by adding three months and dividing by three.

When calculating your income, consider other incomes, such as Social Security, disability, retirement, child support, and dependent benefits. The money you regularly receive can be considered as your monthly budget income.

<u>Monthly payment</u>

It's hard to remember all of your monthly expenses. Start by listing your monthly bills. These include:

- Internet/Cable

- Mortgage and/or rent

- Car expenses: Car fees, insurance, gas, fees, etc.

- Subscription services: gym membership, Netflix, etc.

- Student loan

- Water/electricity/gas

- After listing your monthly bills, add the following variable costs:

- Food: Food and restaurants

- Pharmacies

- Pet costs

The strength of your budget depends on the accuracy of your budget. Look at your credit and debit card accounts for three months to make sure you are getting all the money you normally spend.

<u>Compare income and expenses</u>

Once all costs have been determined, summarize them. What is the price compared to income? Is there excess or lack thereof? If there are surplus, consider how to invest and save the surplus.

If you are in the red, go through your costs and decide what to cut. If lunch at work is one of the biggest leaks, consider packing your lunch in brown bags four days a week. For cable accounts, choose the cheapest plan or shorten the code. Big phone bill? Find a more affordable plan or a cheaper provider. Cost management is not enough. If you can't get what you need, you'll need to count on your income. It may be necessary to work extra hours or find a second job some nights per week.

Your income should always outweigh your expenses. Budget costs should not exceed 90% of the revenue. This is a goal that cannot be reached every month, but that is why you have to back up your savings account. Use emergency funcs only when absolutely necessary, and if you contribute more than your budget, add additional funds within a month.

<u>Budget calculator</u>

Use the budget calculator to quickly reconcile your income and expenses. With Madbu online budget calculator, you can track all your expenses and measure the revenue you need to save money.

<u>How to make a budget?</u>

You can save your budget on paper, but there are many budget applications and software that can help you plan your cash flow more efficiently. Mint is a good online budget tracker, while banks, investment funds, and investment advisors provide their own budget applications. Look around and find the one that suits you.

An important part of the process is tracking the actual cash flow. Save the registry or enter your income and expenses into a computer program. Next, compare the results to your budget. If the price is too high, control it. Remember that your budget is a planning tool, whether it's a paper budget or on a computer or smartphone. You need to take the necessary steps to get the expected result from it.

6. MAKE ADJUSTMENTS TO EXPENSES

Continuous monitoring and adjustment on a budget of costs are essential. In addition to examining costs associated with goals, you can also identify dynamic models or situations that require corrective action. A lot of departments in your budget need procedures to regularly monitor progress towards budgets and goals, usually monthly. In addition, you need appropriate reporting and authentication mechanisms.

Types of information needed to track expenses:

- The annual budget for today's operational and technical specifications overall. When preparing your budget, you need to consider your planned funding methods. For certain types of expenses (especially those that are not related to employees), you can maximize and minimize the expenses at specific points in the year.

- Up to date costs.

- Future cost obligations.

- Annual budget balance. The actual costs and liabilities are compared to the annual budget, and a verification indicates that there is a remaining budget.

- Exposure prediction. This is the expected position on the year-end budget, taking into account all expected costs. Expected exposure is not equal to the initial budget.

- Analysis and interpretation of positive or negative variables compared to costs and projected budgets using a documented action plan to overcome negative deviations.

CHAPTER TWO
HOW TO CREATE YOUR BUDGET WHEN YOU ARE SINGLE

THE FINANCIAL SITUATION OF THE SINGLE

In general, being single means less commitments in more ways than one, so in a lot of cases there are no mortgages, kids' tuition, medicines or family insurance to pay. Everything you enter goes to what the single wants/decides/likes. This can be both an advantage and a great curse. Less financial commitments can have fewer debts; this does not mean that there are no single borrowers, sadly. The income is less. Yes. Married couples where both work and both contribute can expand their wallets. Two are more than one. With honorable exceptions, most singles are young (under 35), and this provides interesting financial advantages.

THE FINANCIAL CHALLENGES OF THE SINGLE

Dominate the crazy spender who lives inside himself. As there are no compromises, it is easy to fall into temptations, overspending on "nonsense." There is no one to check you, but yourself. The younger you are, the more you can fall into the illusion that there is time for everything (I will save in the future), that nothing will happen to us (make sure), and that everything is wonderful. Set priorities. The fine art of setting priorities becomes difficult for singles and married alike, but when you're alone, it's easier to fall into the confusion that your priority is to have fun or buy shoes when many times, your true priority is something else. Two are better than one. For many things, being two increases our portfolio (or prevents the weights from going out). Simply having someone's support to get the dog out when you're sick, for example, and not having to pay someone to do it makes a difference. It is a crude and simple example, but it paints the picture. The flirt. Don't laugh! The money that single men and women likewise spend on the whole process that involves meeting the partner of our dreams can be a small fortune: from clothes, beauty products and gyms, to bars and fashion outlets.

It may seem like life was made for families with children. However, the number of people living alone is increasing. A few generations ago, being single was synonymous with having failed in personal relationships. Today, it is a life option, as respectable as having a partner but more independent and with less attachment. When it comes to saving? How can you save when you are single? In relation to finances, people who live alone have it a little easier to save. By not living with anyone, they can adopt savings measures without giving explanations and without depending on anyone else's opinion. The decisions are only theirs, and they are solely responsible for both their successes and failures. Developing a budget for single and couples requires some same basic steps, which can be modified based on individual choice:

- Get every financial statement you can

- Record all of your income sources

- Create a list of monthly expenses

- Split expenses into two categories: fixed and variable

- Sum your monthly income and expenses

- Make adjustments to expenses

SAVING WHEN YOU ARE SINGLE IS MUCH EASIER: HERE ARE THE KEYS

1. Budget it all

The budget is very important for anyone, also for singles. If you are in a situation where more money comes out of your pockets than you earn, you have no choice but to make cuts. The only way to anticipate the expenses of the month is by budgeting them, and you have the great advantage that you can set that budget based on your needs without depending on anyone else's desires.

2. Control what you buy in the supermarket

Buying in the supermarket is a bit more difficult for singles. Everything seems grouped in large packs to benefit families. You should make a list of what you need and buy thinking about what you are able to consume. Avoid buying products that expire quickly or get in poor condition in a short time, and it is vital to save when you are single. Throwing away food is throwing away money.

3. Freeze food

When you cook, do not prepare just one serving. Take advantage that you are already involved in the task of preparing food for several days. This way, you will take advantage of the complete product and save electricity. Tupperware and the freezer are your great allies to save money. You should also freeze raw meat that you do not consume on the spot or containers that are too large.

4. Take advantage of the offers

You can save a lot of money if you take advantage of offers, such as "50% free," "the second unit at half price" or "take three and pay only 2," especially if it is non-perishable products. If you have a large pantry, you can store water, juice packages, milk, canned cans, shampoo cans, and detergent. Buy them when they are discounted and save them for when you need them.

5. Save on telecommunications

Living alone, you do not need the landline, pay-tv, unlimited calls on the mobile, or 300Mb fiber optic at all. In the case of fiber, you could also consider sharing it with your neighbor. Only one wall separates you, and surely the WiFi signal can work perfectly from one house to another.

6. Avoid whims

In times of downturn, some singles tend to pamper themselves because they believe that this will improve their mood: a new jacket, a new TV, or a new iPhone. These compulsive purchases are very dangerous and prevent them from saving. Associating consumption with happiness is a mistake to avoid at all costs, especially if you are single.

7. Control your social life

Just because you are single does not mean that you should eat dinner outside several times a week, go out almost every day, or go to all the parties you hear about. A busy social life is also a very expensive social life.

Your singleness can help you save more than the people of your age who have already formed a family. If you organize yourself, you can do well by saving and also investing. You may not have to wait to turn 67 to retire. Being financially literate will show you that retiring has nothing to do with age, but everything to do with being prepared. You can retire in your 20's, 30's, 50's or 70's, so the choice is yours.

TAKE ADVANTAGE OF YOUR FINANCIAL ADVANTAGES!

Detected the challenges, here are the advantages that, unfortunately, many wasted:

1. The youth! Save for your retirement from now: The younger you are; the less money you have to remove from your present to expand the bank account of your old self.

2. Buy that apartment: While it is true that you could have more difficulty getting that mortgage loan as a single person, you'll also have more availability to save and allocate a good part of your income for a house without risking important things.

3. Buy your insurance for major medical expenses: You have the resources, so go with the vacation now alone because it will be more complicated later to vacation with four people.

4. Invest: As a single person, you can afford to learn to invest without sacrificing anyone along the way. Buy your mini apartment and learn to be a landlord early on.

Maybe you will like it, maybe you will not like it good, but do it regardless. By the time you have a family, you will already be an expert.

5. Learn personal finances: Singleness is the perfect time to learn, spoil, and experiment before you have more commitments and less time at our disposal.

6. Make financial mistakes without guilt: With learning but without guilt. And promise that you will not commit them again (at least not the same!). To me, singleness taught me that:

- If I don't take care of my money, nobody will do it for me.
- I should have started saving for my retirement when I started working.
- It hurts less to make mistakes when you are the only victim of them.

If you want to take your expenses seriously, there are many applications that can help you easily set a budget and record your expenses at the moment. At the beginning of each year, you set goals and objectives to improve a certain aspect of your life or day to day; lose weight, get fit by doing sports, learn a new language, etc. since you know you are blessed with the total freedom of doing whatever pleases you. One of those goals should be to efficiently manage your money. This is very important as it will determine what the future has in store for you. There are tools that can help you have minimal control over what comes and goes and be able to plan certain things in the medium term with the greatest possible peace of mind. In short, there are tools with efficient management of personal savings. After learning the importance of saving, it is necessary to know how to save and how much to save each month to manage your money to grow effectively. It is a fundamental element in the financial mentoring program, one of the fundamental pieces. Traditionally it has been done in a notebook with paper and a pen. However, this is not usually the most operative due to our scarce resource, time. That's why multiple personal budget management applications have appeared that help us to achieve the goal. You definitely need one to help you manage your finances. If you think you are too busy to do so, there are applications that can make it easier for you:

1. Mint (Best overall): This is the best application to manage your money with more than 20 million users. Mint is one of the most popular personal finance applications in the United States. In addition to being free, with Mint, you can concentrate all your accounts in one place and track and categorize your bank account expenses, credit cards, loans and mortgages, and also your income and investments. This gives you an overview of the state of your finances and allows you to create budgets and know exactly how you are handling your money. Mint also includes options to establish and follow short- and long-term objectives, such as creating an emergency fund or paying certain debts, notification for payment of bills, monitoring of your credit score, and recommendations according to your credit, habits, and financial goals. It is perfect for those who do not have too complicated finances and want to manage them from one place. It is also very useful in reminding you not to forget to pay bills. However, Mint has some constraints as its investment tools are very basic, and many users have problems with the synchronization and

reconciliation of bank accounts. It is not available outside of North America.

2. PocketGuard: This is a multipurpose budget management and account tracking app that shows your account balance and the amount available for the day. The app connects you to your bank account with an encrypted, read-only link, allowing you to quickly track the status of your account and transactions while maintaining security. The app automatically assigns purchases, subscriptions, bill payments, and previous factors, and estimates the amount that can be safely used on your account without entering red numbers.

3. YNAB (Ideal for Type A personas: You need a budget): YNAB follows the cult of avid fans who earnestly call the app YNAB. YNAB has a unique approach to budget submission. Instead of relying on traditional budget deposits, it creates a budget based on your income and assigns work to every dollar of your budget. These jobs include everything from living expenses to debt payments, savings and investments. Leaving the dollars in detail will force you to think about every dollar you spend. This app is perfect for couples working together on a budget. It provides a desktop and mobile interface, the option to automatically synchronize bank accounts, or the option to manually enter costs. It also includes credit payment and goal tracking features and helps you achieve your money goals. Useful for motivation.

4. Wally: This application is available for almost all currencies, so if your work takes you to travel outside the country very often, it is ideal for you, also if you are a lover of savings and travel, here are the best cards to

travel to abroad. It will allow you to save images of receipts, so you can keep track of essential items related to taxes and business without having to deal with paperwork. Each time you log in, Wally will let you know how much money you have and how you can measure it to arrive without constraints at the end of the month. With that information and the ability to manage finances in almost any currency in the world, it is not surprising that Wally is so popular among millennials.

5. Mvelopes (Best for Cash Style Budgeting): This personal budget software is based on the popular concept of creating "an envelope" for each category of budget spending. The difference is that with Mvelopes, your budget envelopes are virtual. Use your income to "finance" your expense categories. There are three levels of Mvelopes available, from the basic level of Mvelopes that only run on your mobile device to Mvelopes Complete, which includes a monthly meeting with a personal finance coach. The free level of Mvelopes limits the number of envelopes you can have, a restriction that does not exist for premium users.

6. Good budget (Best for Couples): An application created by a small team of mortals who want to do something simple about personal finance and for whom money management is something really personal. Like most of these apps, it allows you to define a budget, scan expense receipts, manage money by categories, set savings goals, and visualize behavioral graphs.

7. MadbuMax: An online program that you can access from anywhere to manage your finances. Track your expenses, your sources of income, and keep your eyes

on your accounts at all time. You can use it to track your utilities and how much you spend on them every month. MabuMax was created by me, so as an owner of this book you will have access to this program for free. Just email me for access. Go to madbu.com and go to the contact section to request access.

8. Simple (Best App Tied to a Bank Account): This app has been at the top of the most demanded time to generate ideas. The app allows you to create mind maps following the main idea and choose the one that suits you best. With 8 million users, they represent themselves as the world leaders in cross-platform mind mapping tools. The app also helps you graphically organize your brainstorming and share diagrams with other people. Although there is a free version, they do not offer all the features in it.

9. Personal Capital (Best for Investors): Bank and investment participation, costs, portfolio performance, investment allocation, industry weights, current balances, and even home value are updated. Knowing what happens to your money anytime and anywhere will help you save more and make better investments. This is the only asset and investment management tool you need.

CHAPTER THREE
SAVING FOR EMERGENCY

WHAT IS THE EMERGENCY FUND?

The emergency fund is an amount of money that we must have separated to meet unexpected expenses. You can consider it as a kind of financial lifeguard. Although I have and recommend having most of the assets invested in the stock market, I always have a certain amount of money in liquidity. This allows me to face unforeseen expenses without necessarily having to sell shares or request a loan to get ahead.

In what cases should you go to your emergency fund?

It is important to be aware that the money that's part of your emergency fund should be used only to cover unforeseen expenses that are beyond your control.

Some examples are the following:

- A mechanical breakdown of the car

- A domestic repair

- Suffer a layoff

- The bankruptcy of your company

In no case should you use this money for expenses that you already know you will have to face. If you know that you are going to spend $3,000 every year on vacation, you should not take that money out of the emergency fund since it is a totally predictable expense. Therefore, you should start creating a vacation fund throughout the year, separate from the emergency fund. The same happens with the payment of insurance or the return to school for children.

If you see that, you will have to face a significant expense within a few months, and you do not have enough liquidity, you should ask yourself if you should undo some investment if it is a good time to do so. Another alternative would be to increase your savings coefficient by temporarily reducing your unnecessary expenses.

Why is having an emergency fund so important?

There are two main reasons why you should have an emergency fund. First, to avoid borrowing costs. Covering this type of exceptional expenses through indebtedness implies an additional cost that can sometimes touch the limits of usury. For example, it is common to see interest rates above 15% or 25% on credit cards or personal loans that are advertised on television. In addition, starting to borrow can create vicious circles that have ruined and continue to ruin many families.

On the other hand, the emergency fund will help you avoid selling off your investments at the worst possible time. The times of generalized layoffs usually coincide with significant loss of asset. Not having money available for emergencies can force you to sell shares at the worst time, at a very high cost for doing so when Mister Market is depressed and buys them for a price much lower than its intrinsic value.

How much money should I have in the emergency fund?

There are different theories about how much money should be reserved in the emergency fund. Although there is no single criterion, a fund capable of paying between three and six months of current expenses is usually recommended.

Although this is the general rule, you need to take into account your personal circumstances to determine the money you should have in your emergency fund. For example, for a couple without children, an emergency fund of three months of expenses may be more than enough. On the other hand, for a family where only one of the spouses has an unstable job, it is possible that a six-month emergency fund may even fall short.

How should I manage my emergency fund money?

Emergency fund money must be deposited in a place that meets two requirements:

That you have immediate liquidity; that is, it can be withdrawn at any time without incurring a high cost, and maximum security. We should not seek profitability but minimize the risk to maintain our purchasing power in adverse circumstances.

For example, you can have your emergency fund at:

- Short-term monetary funds

- Current accounts

- Cash

Now you know what an emergency fund is, its importance, where to deposit it and how to manage it, so if you don't have emergency funds, start creating. This will not only prevent extraordinary costs and some of the labor problems that may occur, but it will also help prevent a financial crisis, which could damage property management in the long run.

How to save money for emergencies?

How do you pay for repairs if your car breaks or the water heater stops working? Do you have money for an emergency? Or do you want to pay with a credit card and increase your current debt? Planners and financial advisors often recommend that you have an emergency fund with three to six months of maintenance costs.

However, in reality, only a few can do it. If you are one of them, good for you. Most people will do nothing instead, perhaps mocking the idea of such elusive goals. This is also not recommended. It would be great if we could reach our goal of getting three-six months of care costs for real chronic emergencies like unemployment and illness. However, the most realistic goal is to start small– $1,000– $2,000 to pursue short-term emergency fund goals.

We know that people will be exposed to the possibility of paying these costs. They know they are not focused on their work. They know they are losing productivity. There are reports that this condition makes them sick. People need to save.

But that idea may not help you in an emergency. You may not be able to create an emergency fund overnight, but you can do it a little bit. Of course, these are very difficult times with everything getting more expensive. In the world we live in today, many people find it difficult to save for future use, but I think they have to make it a habit of saving something no matter how small.

"It's not a quantity, it's something you do on a regular basis. It saves people. It's common to hear that there isn't enough money to save." I ask someone, "Do you have any money? Save money on the 10th of every month or the day you get paid." Yes, at the end of 12 months, there is only $12, but this is generally because it is the key to action. In the meantime, get simple cash in your pocket or a purse in a jar. Saving 50 cents a day saves $15 per month or $180 per year. Statistics show that the average household is $90 in various parts of the house. People have not failed because they are struggling to save. Most of us suffer at some point in our lives. The important thing is that you can save a bit. Another important method is to follow the tips for generating dollars and save instead of spending the difference. People who "can't save money without saving the difference" need to define the meaning of an emergency. It can't be, "Look, I'm depressed today. I need to buy shoes." The idea of having emergency funds is to prevent debt growth. If you need to spend it, then fill it up for the next emergency, and you can move on to the next goal of saving three to six months of maintenance costs, equivalent to long-term emergency funding.

You might need to save for a long-time emergency fund, which is already seen in the present. In order to achieve this, you need to have a regular saving with a projection of the appointed time. Your projection savings should not be easy to access by you or your family. It could be three months, six months, and even years of savings. What matters most in this type of saving is consistency.

CHAPTER FOUR

SAVING FOR RETIREMENT

How often do you think about retiring? What is your plan? Is it reachable? For some, it seems complicated to plan for retirement, but for others, it is very far away. The truth is that retirement comes to reality many times faster than we think, and you need to take certain basic steps from an early age to enjoy this long-awaited time without major problems or changes to your lifestyle that can achieve this in a financially secure way. I encourage you to consider some key points for planning your retirement:

Define future plans

When it comes to retirement strategies, there is no specific model for everyone. This depends on the current financial situation and future expectations. These decisions come with certain costs that must be considered, so you need to determine the lifestyle you need when you retire. At what age do you want to retire? Do you live with family or do you live alone? Do you want to travel or join the community more? Answering these and other questions will help you plan your retirement in line with your expectations.

Check your current financial status

It is important to check your current financial situation. This will help you identify the steps needed to achieve a financially safe retirement.

Make a budget

You need to analyze your expenses and create an actual budget for the year. Budgets help you understand your current financial situation and determine how much money you can save and invest before you leave. Also, many experts recommend repaying large debts, such as mortgages and other loans, before retiring, to focus solely on covering daily expenses.

Do you currently have any savings or investment plans?

As part of a retirement plan, you need to save a certain amount and invest in assets that benefit from acceptable risks. People near retirement tend to have a lower risk tolerance, so invest in more conservative measures. We recommend that you consult with your financial advisor to evaluate various investment options, taking into account your risk profile and the time horizon.

Identify your income needs

As soon as you know your current situation and where you want to go, you can tell if you need to take additional steps to meet your retirement goals. As a rule, many experts have shown that 60-80% of current income is required for retirement. Nevertheless, it is desirable to determine each specific income requirement according to the annual assessment of pension costs. This requires adjusting current expenses according to the potential for future lifestyle changes. For example, medical expenses may increase during retirement, or conversely, mortgage expenses may decrease or disappear if the loan is paid in full.

Additional sources of income

After you determine your income needs, determine how much you need to save to close the gap between your current situation and the future you want. There are various additional sources of income that we can consider. Some experts recommend saving 15% of income before retiring. Whether we use this or that method, we have to establish annual savings.

If you are not married before the wedding, it is advisable to save as much as possible. This will help to not delay your retirement date to increase your savings. Another option is to invest some of your savings. As already mentioned, there are investment institutions that offer a wide range of options and pension fund management companies that provide benefits to contributions by deducting them from income taxes.

In addition, some people prefer to move to a small, inexpensive home. This can lead to benefits that contribute to savings after retirement. Another option is to use your home as collateral to request a loan. Credit lines for the value of your home may give you some financial flexibility before retiring. You also need to consider government benefits, such as social insurance and private companies. It is worth noting that for some people, social security is not a source of income and is not a source of income that can rely solely on retirement.

No matter how old you are, it is not too early to begin your retirement planning. Although retirement may seem like a reality for all of us, start this planning process so that you can enjoy a financially prepared retirement

Examples of maintenance plans:

1. Defined contribution system (DC)

After being introduced in the early 1980s, the plan, including 401 (k), nearly occupied the pension market. About 84% of Fortune 500 companies offer DC programs instead of traditional pensions.

Plan 401 (k) is the most common DC plan for employers of all sizes, and plan 403 (b) has a similar structure and is offered to public school employees and some tax-exempt organizations. Project 457 (b) is more accessible to governments and municipalities. Many DC programs offer a version of Roth that uses dollars after tax, but you can get a tax refund after retirement. If retirement tax rates are expected to be higher than donations, Roth's election makes sense.

401 (k) plan

Plan 401 (k) is a preferential tax scheme that provides retirement savings. The employee pays for the project upfront. That is, donations are not considered taxable income. According to Plan 401 (k), these contributions may increase without tax until withdrawn after retirement. After retirement, distributions generate taxable income, but withdrawals before 59 and a half are subject to additional taxes and penalties.

Benefits: Plan 401 (k) is an easy way to maintain your pension because you can automatically invest money from your salary. Funds can be invested in more profitable investments, such as stocks, without paying income tax until the funds are withdrawn. In addition, many employers offer free cash and automatic profits as a decent contribution and only offer savings.

Cons: The main disadvantage of 401 (k) is that you need to pay a fine if you need money in an emergency. Many plans allow you to borrow money for a legitimate purpose, but this does not guarantee that your fund manager will do so. Investment is limited to the funds provided by employer plan 401 (k), so you cannot invest in what you want.

403 (b) plan

Plan 403 (b) is similar to Plan 401 (k) but is funded by public schools, charities, and several churches. Because employees donate pre-tax money to the project, donations are not considered taxable income, and these funds may increase without tax before retirement. Upon retirement, withdrawals are tax-deductible, and additional taxes and penalties may apply if you are 59 and a half or older.

Benefits: A 403 (b) is an effective and popular way to save retirement benefits, and you can plan to automatically deduct money from salaries and more efficiency savings. You can invest money in many investments, including profitable assets, such as pensions and fund funds, without having to pay taxes until the money is returned. If you save money at 403 (b), some employers may offer you appropriate contributions.

Cons: Like 401 (k), funds for plan 403 (b) are difficult to access without qualified emergency assistance. You have access to cash without emergencies but may incur additional fines and taxes, but you can get a 403 (b) loan. Another disadvantage: your options are limited to options for investing in the plan, so you can't invest in what you want.

457 (b) plan

Plan 457 (b) is similar to Plan 401 (k), but it is only available to state and local government employees and certain tax-exempt organizations. This tax effect plan allows employees to participate in pre-tax plans. This means income is not taxed. Up to 457 (b), the pension increases without tax and is taxed when the worker receives the money.

Benefits: Plan 457 (b) is a great way to maintain your retirement for tax benefits. This program provides special savings measures for elderly workers not covered by other programs. Refunds under the age of 59 are not subject to a 10% penalty like on Plan 401 (k). This is because 457 (b) is considered an additional savings plan.

Cons: The regular plan 457 (b) is less attractive than plan 401 (k) because it does not guarantee employer compliance.

2. IRA Plan

IRA. A valuable pension scheme created by the government. By 2020, individuals will be able to donate up to 6,000 with one account, and employees over the age of 50 can donate up to 7,000.

There are many types of IRAs, including Traditional IRA, Roth IRA, spousal IRA, self-directed IRA, rollover IRA and simple IRA. Here is what they are and how they differ from each other.

Traditional IRA

Traditional IRA is a tax credit program that allows you to receive significant tax credits upon retirement. Anyone who works and makes money can make a contribution before cutting taxes. In other words, contribution is not tax-deductible. The IRA provides deductions from these contributions until the account holder is eligible to collect and deduct them upon retirement. Early withdrawal may impose additional taxes and penalties on employees.

Benefits: The traditional IRA is the most popular retirement investment account because it offers valuable tax credits and allows you to buy almost unlimited investments, including stocks, bonds, CDs, real estate, and more. Perhaps the biggest benefit is that you do not have to pay taxes until after you retire.

Cons: If you need money with a traditional IRA, eliminating taxes and additional penalties can be costly. In the IRA, you need to invest in banks, stocks, securities, etc.

The Roth IRA is a new example of a traditional IRA with significant tax benefits. Contribution to the Roth IRA are made after-tax. In other words, you paid taxes on the money you deposited in your account. Instead, you don't need to pay contribution or income tax from your account when you log out.

Spousal IRA

IRAs are usually reserved for paid workers, but the IRA subsidiary pays for the spouse of a paid worker. The taxable income of a working spouse must exceed the contribution of the IRA. My wife's IRA is a traditional IRA or IRA Roth.

Benefits: The biggest advantage of an IRA spouse is that spouses who are not working can take advantage of the various benefits of the IRA.

Cons: There are no specific drawbacks to sub-IRAs, but like all IRAs, you have to decide how to invest.

Rollover IRA

A small IRA is created when a retirement account, such as a 401 (k) or IRA, is transferred to a new IRA account. You can "transfer" from one account to the IRA rollover to use the IRA tax credits. The IRA rollover can be installed in companies with traditional IRAs or loss IRAs. There is no limit to the amount that can be transferred to an IRA rollover.

The Rollover IRA allows you to change the type of retirement account from a traditional IRA to a Roth IRA and vice versa. Create an IRA rollover, deposit money, and send money. However, certain types of transfers may generate tax benefits, so it is important to understand these effects before deciding how to proceed.

Benefits: The Rollover IRA will continue to offer attractive tax benefits if you decide to discontinue your former employer's 401 (k) plan. If you are migrating an IRA provider to an existing IRA, you can migrate your account to a new provider. As with all IRAs, you can purchase a variety of investments.

Cons: As with all IRAs, you need to decide how to invest money. This can be a problem for some people. Special attention should be paid to the consequences of tax on carrying money. This is usually only an issue when changing account types. This is because it can be significant.

3. Non-qualified deferred compensation plan (NQDC)

If you are not a very senior executive, you may forget to offer the NQDC program. But we look forward to them. One looks like a 401 (k) plan with salary cuts and competition, and the other is funded by employers.

The catch is that in most cases, the latter is not really funded. Employers can create "payment promises," create accounting entries, and protect funds, but these funds are subject to lender billing.

Benefits: Has the advantage of saving money on a tax-deferred basis, but employers cannot deduct contributions until they start paying income tax at the time of withdrawal.

Cons: They do not provide much protection. If your company has financial problems, there are certain risks you can't get (from the NQDC plan).

4. Cash balance plan

This is a form of defined benefit and retirement plans. However, instead of replacing a fixed percentage of income over a lifetime, certain virtual account balances are guaranteed based on contributing credits and investment receivables (e.g., annual interest). The most common setting for cash reserves is the company's contribution of 6% salary and 5% investment credit per year.

Investment credits are pledges and are not based on actual contribution credits. For example, suppose you have 5% of income or investment credit. Employers can reduce contributions by earning more in retirement assets. In fact, many companies that wish to cancel a traditional pension plan are switching to a cash reserve plan to better manage the plan's costs.

Benefits: The promised benefits continue to be provided and do not need to contribute. In addition, when changing jobs, the account balance is low, so you can get the previous limit amount.

Disadvantages: If a company switches from a generous pension plan to a cash reserve plan, some companies may retire long-time employees to the original plan, but older workers may lose.

5. Profit-sharing plan

Some companies encourage workers to create profit-sharing plans to help increase and distribute corporate profits. This is another useful advantage that cannot be contributed; only employers can. But here's the problem. Employers have the option to donate annually. However, the government says its contribution is "continuous and substantial."

Pros: There is no cost, depending on the profit-sharing plan. You can choose the investment you need. In other cases, the trustee will process the investment decision.

Cons: Profit-sharing programs are not a safe way to ensure financial security. It is difficult to predict retirement benefits. I don't know how much the company is contributing each year. I don't know what my investment experience is.

6. Central Government program

The Federal Employee Retirement System (FERS) provides a secure three-tier retirement planning platform for individual employees who meet specific service requirements.

Benefits: Federal employees are eligible for defined benefit plans. In addition, you can receive a 5% donation from the employer to TSP. This includes a 1% non-participation contribution, a 3%-dollar competition, and a match with the next 50% 2% contribution. The formula is a little complicated, but if you put 5%, you get 5%. Another good thing is the surprisingly low cost of the investment, 4/100 points. Equivalent to 40 checks. It is much cheaper than anywhere else.

Cons: As with all defined contribution plans, there is always uncertainty about what will happen to the account balance on retirement. What this means for you: you still need to decide how much you want to contribute, how to invest, and how to choose Roth. However, it makes sense to pay at least 5% of your salary for your employer's maximum contribution.

7. Life insurance plan in monetary value

Some companies offer life insurance as a benefit. There are different types: full life, variable life, global life and global variable life. They provide the benefits of death while creating monetary value that can support your retirement needs. The withdrawal of the monetary value exposes the premium paid (in terms of costs) first but is not taxed. The loss of tax processing has some similarities, but it is very complicated. It will not be discarded along the way, but if it is designed correctly, the line can be recovered.

Benefit: Eliminate many risks by providing death benefits or sources of income. In addition, investment growth includes tax deferral.

Cons: If implemented incorrectly, the policy will expire, and you may find yourself too old or unhealthy to get life insurance on your own. Like other insurance solutions that you purchased once, there are some restrictions on your long-term strategy. Another risk is that the products do not always work.

CHAPTER FIVE
INSURANCE OPTIONS FOR YOU

Life insurance

Life insurance helps the moments of your life last. Whether you keep paying the mortgage, maintain the current standard of living, pay off debts in full or pay for college, the life insurance you choose may be there when your loved ones need it most. What is life insurance? Did you know that this acquisition can be fundamental to protect the one you love in the most delicate moment of your life or their life? Every year, we see the drama of families that lose their provider due to an accident or illness. With a few accumulated resources and no life insurance, they need to live with the basic difficulties of financial maintenance – in addition to the pain of grief. Many young men and ladies tend to spend more than $2,000 a year on auto insurance but are hesitant to acquire a life insurance policy into their budget, which can cost less than $100 per month. If that happens to you, it's time to review the priorities.

Is life insurance expendable?

The difficulties of financial planning and the superstitions surrounding death created the mistaken idea that this product was not so important or, worse, that it would bring a bad omen. Meanwhile, in countries like the United States, the volume of citizens protected with this insurance has already reached 59%. Life insurance is a guarantee offered by insurers in which, by means of monthly payments, called "premiums," a person can contract a financial indemnity that will be paid to the beneficiaries in the event of his death, or to himself in several situations provided for in the contract – ranging from serious illnesses to reimbursement of hospital expenses. Life insurance provides for payment of the insured capital to beneficiaries in the event of the death of the contractor. But the common coverage in this type of policy goes far beyond that. They usually provide for compensation if:

Death (whether natural or by accident)

Disability (functional or work, total or partial due to accident or illness); medical, hospital and dental Expenses (DMHO)

- Funeral assistance or assistance
- Serious illnesses or terminal illnesses (such as cancer, acute myocardial infarction, stroke, and myocardial revascularization surgery by means of vascular bridge fixation)

This insurance can also be combined with complementary protection from other products, such as coverage of educational expenses, debt settlement, travel insurance, and home insurance. Realize that this is a mix of protections that goes beyond indemnification to the family.

Nowadays, there is even redeemable life insurance. It is part of financial planning and guarantees redemption after a certain grace period (with interest and corrections).

What are the differences in life insurance?

One of the best-known advantages of life insurance is the Income Tax (IR) exemption, something very rare among the financial products offered by the market. Another benefit is that this product is not considered an inheritance; that is, it does not enter the inventory in the event of the death of the insured. With this, in addition to the release of the money being much faster, there is no obligation to pay the Tax on Transmission Causa Mortis (ITCMD). Life insurance is one of the most effective ways to transfer wealth.

Life insurance can ensure the continuity of your children's educational costs, the settlement of financed properties, or even monthly income to the insured in case of an accident that results in disability. At this point, it is worth mentioning that the contracted capital can be paid in a single payment or in the form of income, depending on what was previously agreed in the contract.

The contracting of life insurance can be individual or collective. In the individual mode, the insurance covers the risks of a single insured, the direct contractor of the plan. Its biggest advantage is being tailor-made, according to age, lifestyle, profession, and coverage of interest. The premium is calculated based on this data and, although it probably costs a little more than in the collective modality, the perfect adaptation of this insurance to your aspirations makes this product interesting.

Collective insurance is provided by a company, association, or union. It will be the one who will negotiate the coverage, guarantees, insured capital, and product format. Whoever signs the adhesion proposal acquires a previously formatted product that, although it is usually cheaper, may not cover their needs as well as individual insurance.

What is the age limit for taking out life insurance?

The insurer calculates the insurance premium (price) based on the risks involved. In the event of death, increasing age increases the risks to the insurance company. Thus, most insurers impose some form of restriction on contractors over 65 years of age. Precisely for this reason, the idea is to take out life insurance as soon as possible – which guarantees the possibility of taking on higher insured capital and with lower premiums. Did you know that it is possible to take out whole life insurance for less than $50 per month depending on the amount of coverage and your health status?

Life insurance, more than a precaution: a matter of responsibility

We must understand that it is part of a set of personal insurance. It is created in order to guarantee the payment of indemnity to the insured and its beneficiaries, according to the contractual conditions and the contracted guarantees. Therefore, before hiring the insured capital, it is necessary to think about some aspects. Who would be responsible for paying funeral or hospital expenses in the event of a fatality, for example? Would any dependent be able to assume these costs?

In addition, how much would it take to pay for your children's private school over a 5-year period? You need to take into account what you want for your dependents in terms of living standards. In the case of a single without dependents, life insurance is not the best option, but disability will be fine for single.

Disability insurance

Permanent disability and the relationship with work. In general, private insurance offers two types of guarantees: basic and additional. When it comes to personal accident insurance, the basic guarantees to be offered are due to the death of the insured or his permanent disability. As an additional guarantee, the insurance must offer temporary disability allowances, which consist of an indemnity for the time the insured is unable to work due to the accident suffered.

Other guarantees that can be offered, depending on the contracted plan are:

- Funeral assistance

- Reimbursement of medical expenses

- Advance payment of the premium due to terminal illness.

It is important to mention that insurance can never be taken out without basic guarantees being offered. CNSP considers a personal accident to be an involuntary, violent event that causes physical injury, which causes the death or permanent, total, or partial disability of the insured. Situations covered by this concept include suicide, or its attempt, accidents resulting from action of ambient temperature or atmospheric influence, when the insured is subject to them, as a result of a covered accident, accidental leakage of gases and vapors, kidnappings and kidnapping attempts and anatomical or functional changes in the spine, of traumatic origin, caused exclusively by fractures or dislocations, radiologically proven.

The following situations are excluded from the concept of the personal accident: Diseases, including professional ones, whatever their causes, even if caused, triggered or aggravated, directly or indirectly by accident, except for infections, septicemic states, and embolisms, resulting from visible injury caused as a result of a covered accident intercurrences or complications resulting from exams, clinical or surgical treatments, when not resulting from a covered accident the resulting injuries, dependent, predisposed or facilitated by repetitive efforts or cumulative microtrauma, or which have a cause and effect relationship with them, as well as injuries classified as Repetitive Strain Injury – RSI, Work-Related Musculoskeletal Diseases – WMSD, Continuous cr Continuous Trauma-Injury – LTC, or similar that may be accepted by the medical-scientific class, as well as its post-treatment consequences, including surgical ones, at any time; and situations recognized by official social security institutions or similar, such as "accidental disability," in which the event causing the injury does not fully fit the characterization of disability due to personal accident. Therefore, work-related illnesses and accidents are not covered by private insurance coverage, and these misfortunes are covered by the benefits granted by the General Social Security System.

Permanent disability due to an accident is covered as an additional guarantee in life insurance. Through this guarantee, the insured person guarantees indemnity proportional to that of the basic guarantee (death), limited to 200% of this, for loss or reduction, total or partial, of the functionality of a member or organ, due to an accident. In cases of permanent disability due to illness, a kind of anticipation of what would be due as a basic guarantee is guaranteed to the insured person who cannot obtain his recovery or rehabilitation with the medical and therapeutic resources available when contracting. Also, in the case of permanent total and permanent disability are those who have terminal illnesses, when certified by a legally qualified doctor.

How to use health insurance?

Health is wealth. Whenever you go to an appointment or undergo an examination or treatment within the agreed network, you will have to pay an amount stipulated in accordance with the terms of the contract. It is called co-payment, the percentage of the cost of the medical care received. There are situations in which you will have to advance the value of the consultation or treatment, for example, if you are using services outside the agreed network of providers. To be reimbursed for this amount, you must send the invoice for the medical act to the insurer, and it will proceed with its reimbursement: the transfer of the amount that is in charge of the health insurance. You should avoid subscribing to very expensive health insurance policies.

Medicare insurance plan: Medicare is a federal health insurance plan. These insurance plans are offered by companies and other private companies approved by Medicare. Medicare Advantage plans may offer prescription drugs that follow the same guidelines as Medicare prescription drugs. The plan is made available for people of;

- 65 and older

- With end-stage renal failure (persistent renal failure, sometimes called ESRT), who require dialysis or transplantation

- Specific young people with disabilities

Medicaid insurance plan: Medicaid is a health plan you can use if you have low income. Children, pregnant women, people with disabilities, and the elderly may be eligible for this type of health plan. Medicaid is a low cost and sometimes free way to get medical care.

Other options include:

- Private health insurance

- Employer-sponsored health insurance

- Other government-sponsored plans

Auto insurance

Did you know different auto insurance companies use different guidelines and standards to rate you? With the same driving record, a company can charge you $500 per month while another one only $100 per month. Always shop around at least once a year or at every renewal. Your wallet will thank you for that. If you have had accidents or infractions in the past, know that in some states they can stay in your record for up to 3 years or 5 years in other states. If you have been with the same company for more than 3-5 years after an accident or infraction, it is time to shop around because your rates could be lower since the company will not automatically re-rate you for a cheaper price.

CHAPTER SIX
REAL ESTATE INVESTING

The real estate sector is one of the oldest and most popular asset classes. Most new real estate investors know this, but what they don't know is how many different types of real estate investments there are. In discovering these different types of real estate investments and learning more about them, it is not uncommon to find references for those who forged the property by learning to specialize in a specific niche.

Types of real estate investment

If you want to acquire, own, or invest into real estate, you can categorize the properties into several categories to better understand what you are facing.

- Residential Housing

A residential structure is a property, such as a house, apartment, villa, and so on. Buildings of 4 units and less are categorized as residential properties, and anything from 5 units and up are considered commercial properties. The lease agreement on residential properties is mostly based on a 12-month contract. There are short-term rentals that will allow for leasing contracts of less than 12 months.

- Commercial

Commercial property typically includes office buildings and skyscrapers. If you take a portion of your savings and build a small building with a private office, you can pay rent and rent it to a company that uses the property or the owner of a small business. It is not uncommon for commercial real estate to engage in multi-year leases. This increases cash flow stability and protects homeowners when rental rates are reduced. The market is volatile, and rental fees can rise significantly in the short term. However, if the old contract blocks commercial real estate, the commission will not be higher.

- Industry

Industrial real estate comes from industrial warehouses, storage units, car washes, or other property for special purposes that generate sales from customers using the facility. Investing in industrial real estate can often generate significant service charges and profits, such as adding vacuum cleaners to car wash coins and increasing the owner's return on investment.

- Retail

Commercial facilities include shopping malls, malls and other retail outlets. In some cases, the owner receives a portion of the sales generated by the tenant's store, in addition to the basic rent, and encourages them to cover their assets.

- Mixed-use

A mixed-use property means to combine any of the above into your project. For example, a Californian investor saved millions of dollars and found a mid-sized city in the Midwest. He looked for a bank to raise money and built a three-story complex office building surrounded by retailers. The bank that paid it earned considerable income for the landlord and borrowed it downstairs. Other sites are rented to health insurance companies and other companies. Nearby stores were quickly rented by a hair salon, quick service restaurant, virtual golf course, sophisticated store, and gym.

Multipurpose real estate investments are popular with people with significant assets because they have a built-in level of diversification that is important for controlling risk.

HOW TO INVEST IN REAL ESTATE

- Buy a property with cash or with a mortgage

- Serve as a middleman between buyers/investors and sellers of properties while earning a finder's fee.

- Flip homes by buying a home at a discount, then rehab this home to resale with a profit.

- Flip contracts by negotiating the price of a property and get it into contract, then find an investor to sell that contract for a higher fee than negotiated. Once everything is set, you keep the profit.

- Become part of an investing group or fund where you may not have to do a lot of work since everyone in the group will be good at something which will make the group stronger. Someone can be good with contracts, another one with insurance, another one with financing, and another one with repair. That way you will complement each other and will reach your investing goals faster.

- Rent a home then list it on different platforms for short term rentals. For example: you can rent a home for $1,000.00 per month, then you list it on Airbnb for 100 a night. If you get it booked 25 nights for the month that's $2,500.00 in revenue from a $1,000.00 investment, and after the fees you can end up with $700.00 – $1,000.00 extra per month. Repeat that with 2-5 homes and that could make you an additional $1,000.00 to $5,000.00 more per month.

In addition, if you do not want to deal with real estate, there are other ways to invest in real estate. Real estate investment funds or REITs are particularly popular in the investment community. When investing through a REIT, you buy shares in a company that has real estate assets and distributes all proceeds as dividends. There are tax issues-your dividends do not qualify for the lowest rate you can get with common stock-but if they are purchased at the right price, they will be a good addition to your portfolio with sufficient coverage. You can also find the right REIT for your industry. For example, a hotel REIT. You can proceed to additional areas, such as a tax lien and more. I will not go too deep into real estate, but if you would like to learn more about real estate investment please contact me www.madbu.com.

CHAPTER SEVEN
SAVING FOR SINGLES WITH A CHILD

How many times have you thought about your children's future? What studies do you want them to have? Or which university are they going to? It does not matter if you are planning to get married next year, or even after ten years, the concern for your children is something that is always there. You might have the intention of giving your children the best in life, but you know there has to be a better way to save for your future, although you don't know very well how to do it. One of the first things you have to consider is for what and when you want to save for your children. That is, for what purpose and for what term? Saving for a summer stay abroad is not the same thing as saving for university. Nor is saving the same with three years of a margin than having more than ten years to do so. And we also have to take into account the Consumer Price Index (CPI) when planning our savings, because the first objective of our savings must be to exceed the CPI every year, so as not to lose purchasing power. Before we look at the different products available to plan savings for our children, we must take into account an initial detail that will make us choose one or the other: Do I already have money saved, or do I need to start saving from scratch? The most effective way of saving is to live the present as the future. Changes are part of everyone's life, and becoming a parent, even when you think you will be single forever, can be one of them. In these situations, it is necessary to have proper financial planning to account for the household bills and the child's upbringing. You can use the 50-30-20 format while preparing your budget. Dedicate 50% of your savings for weekly, monthly, and yearly expenses, while 30% of your savings should be designated for your child/children's future, with the other 20% for emergency purposes. Living in the future today makes the future really issue. There are methods that can help you achieve this with ease and comfort, with or without various financial applications online. You can easily:

Make a family budget

The first thing to do is to create a family budget. Take an online spreadsheet or paper – whichever you feel most comfortable with – and write down all your receipts and expenses. When you look at the numbers and calculate the total you receive and spend, it is easier to see how much you need to save. Therefore, if you spend more than you earn, you will need to prioritize certain items to save on others and evaluate new sources of income. However, if there is money left over every month, it's time to start investing in your emergency reserve.

Create an emergency reserve

The emergency reserve is a guarantee for when you become unemployed, decrease your clients, or have an illness. This way, you avoid using overdrafts or being overdue. The ideal is to add a reserve that allows you to spend at least six months. To do this, organize to invest monthly in this reserve. After all, when we have children, it is common for unforeseen circumstances to appear, and we must be prepared for these cases.

Talk to your child about financial education early

In addition to educating yourself financially, you need to teach your child from an early age how to handle money. As soon as he/she can understand or start asking for toys and other items, start explaining that you can only buy what you can. This is the beginning of the financial education that you will begin to pass on to your child. The older the child gets, it is possible to pass on new knowledge about finance, so you both help each other to keep your budget balanced.

Plan for health spending

When your child is young, it is common for you to spend money on pediatricians, vaccines, and other emergencies. In addition, single mothers and fathers need to eventually take care of their health. Therefore, look for and analyze the hiring of a health plan. Include this spend in your monthly budget, so you have a guarantee for when you need assistance.

Don't forget your well-being

In addition to following all the tips above, it is essential that you also take care of yourself. Being a mother or solo father requires great responsibility and effort. If you do not take time for leisure and self-care, you may be physically and mentally exhausted. Also, have your own goals and dreams. It is not because your child is the focus that you will be left out. So, use money consciously, both to maintain a stable life now and to be able to achieve your financial freedom in the future.

UNIT-LINKED UNIQUE PREMIUM FOCUSED FOR CHILD SAVINGS

These products benefit from a very advantageous tax treatment since they have no contribution limit and only pay for the benefits generated. Its taxation is through Movable Capital Income, which goes from 19% of the first 6,000 dollars of benefit to 23%, if you get more than $50,000 of benefit. They work through portfolios of several investment funds, which makes their behavior and profitability fairly balanced, being able to obtain an average return of more than 7% per year. If instead, you have no money saved, and you're starting from scratch, I recommend the following tools:

CHILD SAVINGS ACCOUNTS

These savings accounts are used to accumulate money for your child, but above all, they must focus on the short-term, since their profitability is usually lower than the CPI. Therefore, these savings accounts are interesting but always linked to the short-term.

College savings plan (529 plans)

These plans are great plans to start saving early for your child's college education. There is a student loan crisis in this country, and you want to be a responsible parent by setting your child up for success at an early age. You can start them for a low monthly premium, and they provide great benefits for your child's college tuition. Speak with a benefits advisor or a financial advisor for more details about how to start one of those for your child.

CHAPTER EIGHT
BUYING A HOUSE WHEN SINGLE

Buying an apartment or house is the dream of the vast majority of people in society today, especially when they are planning to leave the life of singles. But buying your property when you are already married can often be more complicated than for singles. This is because life as a couple or a family involves many costs and/or a higher standards of living compared to someone not married. Therefore, starting to invest in an apartment before getting married is the best option.

You can plan calmly

Saving to buy an apartment before getting married allows your personal and financial planning to be done much more calmly and assertively. In addition, buying an apartment when you are single can favor lighter planning without so many sacrifices. After all, in this phase of your life, there is no urgency to have your own roof so quickly. Married couples who have not had the opportunity to plan before saying "yes" usually need to buy a property with smaller resources. And this question can, in addition to impairing or prolonging any goal, make a life together much more stressful. It is even possible for you to acquire a property on the floor plan, the value of which is lower in relation to the finished property. This is because you will not be in a hurry to move, and you can wait for the delivery of the keys.

You are not the financial person in charge of the family

This is an obvious question, but it is worth emphasizing! Doing financial planning is much simpler when you are not the financial person in charge of the house. Thus, at this stage of life, it is much easier to save money than when you already have a family. When you get married, you need to be aware that responsibility increases, and so do living costs! Keeping the house, taking care of children, and spending on them need financial planning and control. This is also true for those who no longer live with their families but live alone. For even those who live alone and do not yet have a family, saving is much simpler than being married. So, take advantage of this current stage with fewer responsibilities to save and buy an apartment with more peace of mind.

Getting funding can be easier

We all know that it is not always possible to buy a property in cash, with financing being the option of many. However, the entry to start negotiations and buy an apartment is necessary. Remember: the sooner you start saving money to buy an apartment, the higher the entry fee will be. And so, it will be much smoother to pay the financing, and you can pay off your debt more quickly.

Thus, it is worthwhile to strive for the amount to be financed to be as small as possible because the lower the financed amount, the lower the interest payment and the final debt value will be. You can also use mortgage estimators or calculators on sites like Zillow.com, madbu.com, trulia.com and more.

You can analyze spending more carefully

Saving and rethinking your expenses is a more straightforward task when you are single. Unlike married life, when many expenses are considered essential, reducing costs is easier for unmarried people. In addition, giving up buying a good or selling some may not be synonymous with enormous sacrifices. Thus, the idea is to save money when single since the financial impacts on your life are relatively minor. It can be faster and easier to assume the costs of buying a new apartment and prepare for a new phase by analyzing each decision calmly.

Costs for singles are lower than for married couples

Usually, after getting married, you've got the expenses of the children's school, school supplies, and children's clothes. Obviously, your salary will not be used to a large extent for personal needs and wants. Therefore, taking the opportunity to plan the purchase of the first apartment before going up to the altar can guarantee a marriage with fewer worries and more resources to accomplish other goals.

Now that you are aware of the importance of having a house when you are single, you will need to prepare for your family, although you might not be ready to get into marriage in the next few years. You must be aware that:

#1. Living alone does not mean living in a condominium.

Not long ago, anyone who was going to buy a house on their own would immediately look for a kitchenette in a building with many benefits (laundry, housekeeping, etc.), due to the facilities that singles preferred. In addition, condominiums still give their residents the advantage of not worrying about such details as facades, infrastructure, lawns, and lighting in common areas.

Today, this is no longer an indisputable truth. Today, people are looking for other opportunities, which include:

- Free space to allow future expansion of the property for children, companions, etc.

- Extra rooms and rooms for rent, set up a home office, or even receive visitors.

- Have free space for dogs, cats, and other animals.

- Today, with real estate in the central regions skyrocketing, the more distant, bigger, and cheaper real estate spaces have been drawing the attention of buyers.

#2. Do property inspections and demand guarantees

A large part of the issues that scare us when it comes to buying a property is the risks around things that can go wrong and get out of control. People are afraid and do not know, for the most part, what to do when something goes wrong with the house. Often, problems hidden in homes and apartments can put buyers in tricky situations. There are some tools you can use to your advantage when it comes to tackling risks. First of all, property inspections are very useful for this. They cover and prevent any type of fatal flaws in which the transaction may be linked. If you are thinking of buying a house, see the inspection as an opportunity to spend a few more moments in the house, discovering its imperfections, before moving on with the business. Thus, you are aware of the situation of the property and know the condition of the house or apartment you intend to buy, avoiding unwanted surprises.

3. Consult experienced professionals before buying property

Often, you are single but are thinking about buying a property in inventory, sharing the purchase with a friend and/or relative, and even with a partner. This alternative may even seem like a great way to buy a better or more expensive property. But is that a good idea? Buying together or buying a property with problems may even seem advantageous at the moment, as it is less expensive, but it may become a stumbling block in the near future. If you choose to buy a property under any of these conditions, take the time to seek information on how to proceed and how to resolve problems and contingencies in advance to avoid conflicts later. Consulting qualified professionals never hurt, and information about legal conditions for purchasing real estate is always important. When we talk about qualified professionals, we are referring to a lawyer. And the lawyer, and not any other professional, is the person qualified to tell the real situation of a property. That is why you should never acquire property without first talking to a lawyer. After all, it is much easier to invest time in knowledge than to waste money on decisions made inadvertently. Only buy the property after receiving all the pertinent information. Never buy a property on impulse. It is very important to have all the relevant information before choosing to purchase. Buying a property is a relatively large debt, regardless of whether you are financing or buying in cash, so your purchase needs to be made based on research and information. The investment of time in information to make the best decision is always valid, and learning will help you in the future with problems and new investments. Never immerse yourself in buying a home without information or motivated by desire.

PART 2
FINANCIAL PLANNING WHILE ENGAGED

A world's view

According to Ross[5], it is usually crucial to discuss one's finances with their partners. Money can be difficult topics for many couples or dating individuals and it can build or destroy a relationship. For engaged individuals, money can be very tight and understanding personal finances can help prepare in the long term, whereby it helps surface and resolve any issues that may affect the future marriage. When dating, financial planning comes down to communication and each person should be able to prepare a budget, track expenses and income. If being single is a time to build a foundation, the dating period teaches one how to cope with the set foundation and preparing oneself or larger and newer challenges.

Having enough knowledge and understanding of personal finances during engagement can help them agree and determine their spending patterns e.g., buying expensive jewelry or automobiles. It can also help the couples to make decisions on some of the biggest transitions in life, such as getting married or even becoming homeowners.[6] When single, one only needs to worry about themselves and can easily decide to spend less or more, but when engaged, you have to consider other personal decisions. When both couples understand their personal finances, they can be more efficient with their finances in a way that will help them accomplish

---

[5] Ross, Donald Bruce, Catherine Walker O'neal, Amy Laura Arnold, and Jay A. Mancini. "Money matters in marriage: Financial concerns, warmth, and hostility among military couples." *Journal of Family and Economic Issues* 38, no. 4 (2017): 572–581.

[6] Ross, Money matters in marriage, 576

more goals together in the future. More importantly, they agree to work towards their financial stability together.

As an individual, you are able to set the basics for your financial plans when single and when engaged, it is a good time to reevaluate the increase of the earning power. Understanding of the personal finances makes it easier for the dating couples to create a definite plan for their marriage, retirement and also jointly focus on contributing a certain amount for the finance growth.[7]

Additionally, a good understanding of personal finances can help couples to manage and review their income easily. With a proper plan, the couple can be able to effectively decide how their income can well be managed after marriage. Also, they will be able to review and understand their individual allocation among different types of investments that they should invest in the future and align important investment decisions with the lowered time horizon and risk tolerance.[8] During the period of dating, it is also an essential time to check and reevaluate the emergency funds and ensure that they have 3-6 months' worth of personal income that should be saved for future use.

---

[7] Banthia, Dhananjay, and Sujata Mangaraj. "ALiterature Review on Financial Literacy–APathway for Achieving Financial Freedom." *Siddhant-A Journal of Decision Making* 17, no. 1 (2017): 98–102.

[8] Gunardi, Ardi, Mochammad Ridwan, and Gugum Mukdas Sudarjah. "The use of financial literacy for growing personal finance." *Jurnal keuangan dan Perbankan* 21, no. 3 (2017): 446–458.

CHAPTER NINE
HEART TO HEART FINANCIAL TALK

You should start discussing the topic of complex finance if you have ever been financially wrong in the past, or if you don't have knowledge about how your relationship works. We realize that financial discussions are not particularly romantic, but we need to be transparent about finance. Secretly initiating a marriage does not support trust, and inevitably, secrets are discovered at some point.

Create a lively, open, and peaceful space

If you are open and calm when discussing finances, you can be brave, understanding, or willing to accept the situation you or your partner needs to solve. You need to do some work to improve your knowledge when it comes to reporting financial problems and finding ways to collaborate, and there are many topics that can help you understand economically compliant areas. Creating financial goals provides a clear vision and helps establish expectations.

- Understand where you are now as a financial pair.

- Know how you want to manage your finances.

- Compare how funds are handled and managed.

Understand that any financial situation can cause anxiety and other problems if you or your spouse are exposed to them. This will give you a clearer picture of your current situation, your personal limits, and your expectations of what type of financial commitment you would like to buy or retire in the future. Here are some important topics to consider when communicating about your financial problems and learning how to work together.

Talk about the financials of the past

Talk about your habits, duties, obligations and financial thinking about money. Talk about what you think about money and how you managed it in the past. How would you like to keep your finances and how successful or "unsuccessful" are you? Talk about how you deal with money and what's important to you about these experiences. For example, the poor may worry if they don't have savings or spend too much to cover it. If you grow up happy with your finances, it can be difficult to figure out how to budget or borrow. Remember that you must be tolerant, non-judgmental and supportive of your partner's ideas, expectations and financial problems. Please understand that all of us have anxiety-provoking points when it comes to finances. We all have behaviors that are considered excessive, reckless, pathetic, exaggerated and overly protective. Understanding this can help a couple adopt their position and deal with some of these issues.

Your communication about money affects your relationship with your partner.

The way money is communicated can have a significant impact on how you communicate and interact with your finance operations. For example, if your partner is not interested in spending, and you are too cautious, do not get angry or blame your partner when explaining something that happened. Instead, calm down and approach the situation, ask why it happened, and then ask what your partner should do to prevent this in the future. Then plan to address this situation and pursue it. This approach is more informative and practical than expressing the emotions of the situation. Partners (or both) can think that they need to always cover their actions with their wife or husband's money because secret actions or guilt about money and finances are deeply ingrained in one's belief system. Recognizing this problem and developing strategies on how to maintain open financial communication can help find ways to return to the right place when old patterns and patterns break out, and there's debate and distrust. Save a lot of time and energy!

Budget dealings

Budgets are a great tool for communicating about financial issues and learning how to work

together. If you prioritize your budget over financial issues, you will know where you are and agree on what you need and expect financially. The key to maintaining your budget is to review your expenses and change your budget continuously. When budget and financial conversations are open, you can track where you are in relation to your financial goals, and new savings and costs are recognized and negotiated. You can also create the challenge of having more creative ideas about who can save more by investing in grocery shopping or your monthly budget.

Interesting experience

The fun part of working together in financial management is losing the budget and making the experience interesting. This training is a great way to increase each other's commitment, trust and motivation and create mentality for growth and wealth. Consider your budget, not just your household budget, and be sure to consider your personal financial responsibilities.

Maintain good financial habits from the beginning of the relationship. Don't spend money on nonsense, save for emergencies, and have a positive attitude towards money. If one does what is right, it will set an example for the other. Get in touch with relatives and friends whose success story is admired. Talk about money whenever you can, especially together. Dialogue is essential to level expectations and responsibilities, in addition to allowing decisions to be widely discussed and evaluated. The couple should have a monthly budget conversation, as it is impossible to know the family's financial limits without controlling how much money goes in and out. This prevents problems, such as the husband being indebted to the overdraft and the wife continuing to spend by ignoring the problem or vice versa. Create financial commitments for each family member. All responsibilities and decisions should not be concentrated on the man or woman alone. If you have teenage children, ask them to go to the bank to pay bills, even if it is with the money of the father and mother. Sharing obligations with everyone shows the importance of these commitments.

Set common short-, medium- and long-term goals. Money is not just for immediate spending, but it is an important tool for making dreams come true. The human being is naturally individualistic. When forming a family, you must remember that the decisions must be joint. Usually, the purchase of the car is left to the man; however, the financial impact falls on the whole family. It is fair that everyone has an opinion if it is time to change the car and for which model. Make investment a habit, don't wait to be left to invest. Take advantage of technology (online banking) and always schedule the investment the day after receiving the salary. If financial problems arise, look for the solution together, not the culprit. Face the problem together and decide what each person's responsibility will be to change the situation. There are couples who go to extremes. They just want the good part of the wedding but nothing more. They are like best friends sharing the same roof, and they don't want the responsibilities. They think like this: I'm bald, so I don't need to buy shampoo, that's up to her. This kind of attitude does not resolve the situation. Many couples with financial problems choose to separate, but this is not the best way. If couples don't try to resolve all their problems together, they will have challenges, which might result in greater problems, which may eventually lead to a breakup between the couple. Issues, such as debt, will not be resolved and will create an avenue where the marriage is over, but the debts still continue. If there is love and complicity, it is best to try to find a solution together.

CHAPTER TEN
WARNING FINANCIAL SIGNS TO MAKE YOU RETHINK YOUR RELATIONSHIP

Partners do lie about their financial situation. This may seem inappropriate, for example, how to fake more than the amount spent on a dress, or hide the amount of money or debts earned. Lying is a precedent for a marriage that you do not want to deal with. Bad financial situations can arise when partners lie to each other about customs, credit cards or other situations. It is important that your partner be sincere or truly hurt your relationship. Another problem that may be enough to rethink your relationship and how you handle money is addiction. It may be an addiction to drugs and gambling, but it can also be a dependency on purchases. Such actions can really affect your finances, and it does not take long to destroy years of economy and zeal. If you or your partner are struggling with any of these problems, you should definitely seek advice together and individually. Some people want to split up everything 50 percent. They are very value-oriented and are only willing to pay the exact amount of the bill. This can be difficult, as, over time, the focus is on the number of x needed to achieve each goal. It may also be unfair if one of the spouses earns much more than the other, but the other wants to divide everything exactly in half. If this sounds complicated when there are only two people, it only gets worse if you have children. You should definitely seek advice and try to share your expenses in accordance with the 50/50 income ratio. Another problem that may arise is that one of the spouses is trying to control the other spouse with the help of money and benefits. This is much more common in those who have a spouse who is at home to manage the house or take care of the child. It's good when someone deals with financial matters, but decisions must be made by the team. It can be difficult to identify this problem until financial unity is consolidated, in which case, you can seek advice before the situation becomes overwhelming or serious. In a marriage, everything should be considered ours, and one of the spouses should not stop the decision of the other spouse.

It is important that both spouses are ready to collaborate on budgets and plans. Some people only start when they marry a person who has never planned and created a plan, has a budget and considers this plan important. In this case, you are looking for someone who will work with you. This means that your spouse has never had a budget, but if you are going to try this, it is normal. If you refuse to do this, you may need to report your finances and seek advice so that you can find a good way to put together a long-term plan. This can make a huge difference in your success in managing your money. In order for you to have a peaceful relationship with your spouse and with your finances, you need to:

- Analyze the burden of debt you can have

- Analyze all the assets you own

- Understand your savings and spending habits

- Let your dirty clothes out, which means bearing it all to your spouse (including your past financial behavior)

- Discuss your perception about money

- Keep your relationship by spending time together

Your financial success is very important, and so is your relationship. You need to find a good compromise between you and your partner to prevent any tricks, which could lead to divorce and further regrets. Avoid:

- Lying About Financial Situations

- Addictions

- Yours and Mine Attitude (individuality)

- Controlling Through Money

CHAPTER ELEVEN
BUDGET FOR TWO

Throughout their lives, the couple will have to make a series of financial decisions, such as buying or renting a property, living in the countryside or a big city, traveling abroad or within the country, saving for the future, and the best time to change their car. Within this family context, it is necessary to choose priorities together and also act together to make it work. One of the main problems that arise in a couple's life is when one hides the other's financial situation. For example, a couple who were sunk in debt, but the husband refused to tell the woman he owed more than six months on the overdraft. She maintained the standards of shopping and luxury with no worries about children and household bills, and dating, ballads, restaurants, tours, movies and trips cost money. How then, to deal with finances without compromising the couple's happiness? For many people, money has always been and will always remain a subject of discussion and exchange (sometimes stormy) in a couple. Here are some avenues that can be explored by spouses.

Bank accounts

It is sometimes easier to use a joint bank account specifically for joint expenses, such as groceries, mortgage, taxes, electricity, joint projects, etc. The surplus remains in everyone's personal account, which each person can manage. Thus, restaurant expenses between friends, outings to the spa, and ultimately, the contribution to the IRA and the or personal insurance, will be made from the individual account of each spouse.

The placements

Everyone should make their investments individually, according to their investor profile. Each spouse may have a different risk tolerance and different goals. It's better to invest as well. Two main models exist for managing expenses between partners: sharing expenses and pooling of income and expenses.

Sharing expenses

Sharing expenses ensures that spouses can contribute to common expenses in an equal way, if the incomes are similar, in proportion to their salary, or if there is a disparity between the incomes. Example: A couple in which one of the spouses earns 70% of the salary will assume 70% of the common expenses. The excess income, once the common expenses have been paid, will go to everyone.

Pooling income and expenses

With this model, the couple's income is pooled, and all expenses, both common and individual, are assumed from the sum of the income. You will understand that the trust between the spouses must be present so that neither of the two partners feels injured. Ideally, both partners should have a similar vision of managing their finances and value for money. For couples who adopt to pool, it might be important to clarify certain points in the context of financial planning. If you are married, the family patrimony law applies. Thus, many assets accumulated during the marriage (house, cottage, furniture, family cars, money accumulated in pension funds, etc.) could be shared in the event of the breakdown of the union. For de facto spouses, the situation is different; there is no family heritage that holds together! Imagine that one of the two common-law partners have always made major household purchases, such as household furniture. In the event of a break-up, it is quite possible that the same spouse claims possession of the furniture during the separation of the property. What will be left for the spouse with the lowest income? In such a situation, it would be better to plan in advance how the property will be shared using a common living agreement. The cohabitation agreement, also known as a de facto spouse's agreement, is a document in which the sharing of expenses, the sharing of responsibilities and contributions of each member of the household, the manner of sharing property in the event of a breakdown, etc. is provided for. The spouses can indicate what they want in this agreement, and it can be notarized or not.

The relationship with money

The relationship you have with money can come from your education, your family values, or your life course. This is partly why it can be complex and emotional to discuss the issue. Either way, it's important to be aware of your relationship with money first. Are you the anxious type, who does not want to spend money on nothing, or rather the "money is a means of exchange" type, and it must circulate since abundance is made for you? Once your relationship to money has been clarified, the financial advisers suggest taking the time to discuss with your spouse each other's vision and try to find common ground, or at least mechanisms that allow two partners not to feel aggrieved. There is no one-size-fits-all solution in this area, but open and frank communication generally allows both partners to feel more understood and respected in their relationship with money.

Financial education for children will depend on your relationship with money. If your vision is different from that of the spouse, it will become important to discuss it as a couple. Again, open communication between spouses will determine the values for money that you want to pass on to your children.

Seek balance

In fact, the world is no longer the same, and relationships have changed a lot. This means that the man is no longer the one who always pays for everything. The woman conquered her space, entered the job market, and now, also has her responsibilities at the time of accounts. It is not good for the couple if only one of the two pays the entire bill because the person will be overwhelmed, and dating can be seen as an expense and even rethought. Where one person in the couple earns more than the other, that is, the rents are not balanced, there is nothing wrong with the most affluent making the largest disbursements. On trips, for example, that person could pay for air tickets and the hotel.

Compare income

When sharing bills with a partner, each pays half the bill, and each spouse makes a split, which contributes equally to the cost. However, this approach only works if both parties have the same income. If you currently make $5,000 a month, your partner earns $2,000 a month, and if your sharing costs reach $2,000 a month, that doesn't mean halving your bill. This approach allows a partner to spend half of their income on household expenses and only 20% of the other income, which is not fair.

Divide accounts

A fairer way to split bills is for each partner to pay a percentage according to each other's income. If one, of the two partners, contributes 70% of the total income from the relationship, this is the percentage that he or she must pay from the bills. This strategy ensures that there is sufficient cash flow to cover household expenses and allows each spouse to have extra income for personal expenses and investments. Couples who practice this can, for example, open a joint savings account to realize their future dreams and even buy goods together–from a simple video game to a property, perhaps a car.

The division of common goods at the time of separation must follow the principles of society. That is, the sharing must take place in the proportion spent by each one for the acquisition of those goods. If the contribution was equal, the same should happen with the division of values. Now, if one has given 30% and the other 70% of the asset's value, the division should occur in the same proportion.

How should brides break down expenses?

In addition to dividing the accounts according to each other's earnings, a percentage of each other's salary must be set aside for the marriage and the couple's joint life. Set percentages of salary to be saved. In this way, the division becomes more just.

How should married people spend expenses?

Married persons must leave all accounts in the proportional division, and separate percentages for future investments, savings, and investments in the children.

Shared account features

When operating a shared cost account, everyone contributes a certain percentage and pays all invoices. Having a shared expense account means that the couple knows that they have proper communication. The account must always have enough money to cover the costs, and you need to trust that your spouse does not deviate from the agreement of the account.

Talk about finances with your partner

In talking about the subject, the couple prevents each one from feeling exploited or the other ashamed to touch the subject. Remember that money is one of the elements that mostly generates wear and tear in relationships, so when finances are not going well, it is natural for the couple to fight and for accusations to occur. When there is financial harmony, these problems are avoided.

Single people can spend their money in their own way and have their own financial management, but when they are in communion, living a life together and looking for a common direction in the future, the subject of finance must be present. It is very important to know how the other deals with money. Each person has their own "Financial DNA," which is influenced by different family, social and educational contexts. Practice financial loyalty and always share information about your financial reality, income, expenses and dreams.

CHAPTER TWELVE
JOINT OR SEPARATE ACCOUNT

Now that you have a life in common, should you also have the money in common? Here are some ideas that can help you decide the direction of your finances and how to talk about it. Joining two lives in marriage does not always mean joining bank accounts. So, it is good to decide how you are going to manage your money and talk about this matter as uncomfortable and unromantic as it may seem. Know that money is one of the main reasons for the separation of many couples, so it is important to know what each of you wants and expects from the financial part of your life as a couple. After all, there are always two parts and sometimes different salaries as well as different perspectives on how to save or spend money.

Keep in mind that each option presented here requires a conversation and reflection about it. This may take some time, so do not expect to discuss this during a movie break. Keep in mind that each option has advantages and disadvantages, so it is just a question of what will work in your specific case. Whatever you decide about your finances can always be changed and adapted to the reality of the moment. It is always advisable to review your ideas during the wedding, as both income and expenses change over time, and certain changes, such as having children, buying a house, an unexpected illness, can change the objectives set initially.

JOINT ACCOUNTS AND SAVINGS

Benefits

This option is a kind of declaration that your lives are shared, not only in love but also in financial terms. All your money is in the same bag, so all bills are paid from the same bag. This option is as simple as possible; there does not have to be transfers between bank accounts, or the need to decide who pays what, when the money that comes into the account belongs to you both. This option implies a relationship of great trust, transparency and responsibility.

Disadvantages

Who will be responsible for the money and its movements? A joint account requires a high level of communication and honesty between the couple. In a joint account, there is no place for privacy, and all expenses and savings are visible to both. If one or both of you are very independent people, this solution may not be the most recommended. If you do not have a similar income, resentments may begin to exist, and one of you may begin to feel aggrieved, so it is necessary to know if you are prepared for such an outlook.

How to talk about a joint account

As a couple, you must emphasize the fact that the relationship is a union at all levels: loving and financial. You must be sure that it does not matter who wins more or less and that there is no "mine or your money;" there is only "our money." Although both share the same money, they must first decide what amount each month can be used for superfluous and fun things, so that the later one does not feel resentful of the other's expenses. Decide who will be responsible for paying the bills.

There is one who is usually more interested in this task than another, but in the end, it is very important to define how both partners deal with money and where it should go.

SEPARATE ACCOUNTS AND SAVINGS

Benefits

The option of having separate accounts and savings allows for a sense of independence, with no need to worry about each other's financial decisions. This option also becomes a fairer option as expenses can be divided according to each person's income. The separate accounts and savings allow for financial autonomy, each having a different banking history.

Disadvantages

There is no control over the money each has, nor whether the bills are properly paid, or whether each partner is saving an equivalent amount. There is less communication because if you do not have joint accounts, there is no need to talk about your joint financial objectives. If there is an urgency, and one of you needs to access the other's account to make an urgent payment, it will not be possible to do so.

How to talk about separate savings and accounts

Couples who choose this route are people who are usually used to managing their own money, so this type of conversation becomes more like a set of ideas, like who pays what, and what amount they should save. In this case, they usually agree that each person should be responsible for their own expenses, or divide the accounts based on each person's receipts. They can, however, share expenses equally, or not, but avoid getting into details, such as, "if you eat instant soups, then I don't pay for soups," as this will be a source of great resentment and sign of little balance in the relationship. Talk about your financial goals, including savings; although the accounts are separate, there will be common goals, like how to buy a new home.

MIXING JOINT AND SEPARATE ACCOUNTS

Benefits

This solution may be the most suitable, as it is a moderate option. Each of you can maintain a degree of independence, but you will both feel that you are contributing to a common goal. This option is more flexible as joint accounts do not have to be used only to pay expenses; they can also be used to make investments, vacation savings, etc.

Disadvantages

A larger number of accounts can make finances more difficult to manage as they require more management skills from both parties, as well as more maintenance expenses. It may also be more difficult to maintain control over the financial landscape with regard to expenditure and savings.

How to chat about a mix of joint and separate accounts

As this situation implies at least three different accounts: one belonging exclusively to each one and a joint one, both ideas implicit in the conversations about the previous options should be applied in a conversation of this nature. In this type of agreement, there must be a degree of trust about the type of bank accounts a couple intends to have and the way they manage money. There is often one person who manages money better than the other, and, in this case, it may be the best of both worlds.

However, you should not mention the fact that one of you does not know how to manage money so well: focus on the advantages of such a solution, commit to giving feedback to each other about managing the joint account. If only one of you is in charge of managing the joint account, you should give the other feedback about your management.

CHAPTER THIRTEEN
FINANCIAL PRIORITY

When it comes to budget, you are in a tremendous conflict when analyzing your goals and realizing that not everything has been going as planned. This is due to the great difficulty in establishing priorities: is it more worthwhile to increase the contribution to the pension plan, or to pay a larger portion of an outstanding debt? Is it better to pay off your car if you can?

Step 1. Pay your debts

No matter how much your intention is to invest, it is useless as long as you have debts to pay. Depending on your degree of debt, this can be a difficult objective to achieve. Thus, it is best to establish priorities in the payment of debts. Not all debt needs to be paid in one go. After all, what you must establish is your financial balance, right? There are no problems in financing the purchase of some goods, but if the expenditure on installments already consumes more than 30% of your budget, it is time to set this debt reduction as a priority.

Step 2. Make it a habit to save

At any time, it is important to have control over your financial life and honor all your commitments. Always spend less than you earn to have financial balance, and pay your bills on time, so you don't lose money on fines and interest. Check alternatives to save and thus reduce costs: review your grocery list, eat more meals at home, search for prices and negotiate payment terms. Take a good look at how you consume. Stop and think before buying something, "do I really need to buy this product? Do I have enough money for that? What impact will this purchase have on my budget?

Step 3. Set up a financial reserve

Once the habit of saving is cultivated, it is time to pursue greater financial tranquility. You are ready to set up an emergency reserve! The accumulated resources must be equivalent to the period of three to six months of current expenses and are intended to guarantee their survival in case something unexpected happens. The best way to achieve this goal is to invest all the extra money you earn, which includes the money you received from the thirteenth or holiday bonus, or even the income tax refund.

Step 4. Plan for the future

The secret to good financial planning lies in the balance between fulfilling your day-to-day obligations, saving for the fulfillment of dreams, and planning your retirement. There are several investment options for those looking for the long-term. You should find out about them and choose the one that best fits your profile as an investor. Since contributions to pension plans allow income tax deductions up to the limit of 12% of your gross annual income, it may be worth investing up to this amount every year to benefit from the advantageous tax treatment.

Step 5. Pay off your real estate financing

For those who have already high real estate debt, but now have a more balanced financial situation, this may be the time to review the terms of the financing. Who knows, you may not be able to afford a larger installment, in order to pay off your debt faster. A quick and effective tip on paying your mortgage is to pay it every two weeks instead of once a month. When you pay that way, you'll end up with 26 half- payments per year which is a total of 13 payments when 12 is required. This simple strategy can help you pay your mortgage 5 to 7 years faster.

Step 6. Think about the family

If you have dependents, you need to think about their future. Start by taking out life insurance, which gives you some financial security in the event of your death. Other options are personal accident and unemployment insurance. After all, you don't want them to have to drop out of school because you got fired, right? Since thinking about your children should be your priority, why not add a reserve to pay for their studies, or guarantee resources if they start their own business?

Step 7. Keep saving and enjoy life

Saving is a habit that you must cultivate throughout your life. But now that you've achieved all of the above goals, it s time to enjoy life and have fun!

THE PROS AND CONS OF RENTING A HOUSE

Renting one or more rooms of the same house is, nowadays, a very common practice against the lease of the whole house. However, in these cases, the contract is regulated by the civil code and not by the law of urban leases since only part of the house is being rented. Thus, the room rental is not covered by the guarantee system established by the law for both the lessor and the lessee. The landlord must make a contract for each of his tenants. The duration of the lease is the one established by the parties, there is no mandatory extension system, and the most usual is that it is set for the school period, in the case of students. The rent for rooms has to be given in furnished housing, so it is necessary to establish a list of the furniture of the common areas and of the room that is rented. In addition, rules on the use of common areas should be reflected.

In the rents of habitual housing, the owner of the property has greater tax advantages (he is exempted from paying the taxes, although he must declare the benefits that he obtains for the lease of the house, which can be reduced between 60% and 100% of the rental price in the income statement). If you decide to rent your home for rooms, you will have to declare the income from the rent, although you can deduct for it. Of course, the tenant has no right to any relief

On the other hand, there are several cons of this contractual modality for the owner:

First, there is the term set by the parties, not subject to the three years established by the law for complete housing. The problem arises with certain groups, for example, students usually rent for the school period, so in the summer months the room is not leased, and, in addition, the owner does not have the security of re-renting it to the next year.

Second, there is the fact of having several contracts with different people in which the rules of sharing the house and the common areas between them come into play, while in the rental of the house, it is the responsibility of the lessee to choose the person with whom he lives. In this case, it is the responsibility of the owner to sign the contract with each of the tenants.

Finally, the issues of responsibility come into play: in the case of the lease of the house, the responsibilities of the lessee and the landlord are clear, while in the rental of the house by rooms, we find the responsibility of each one of the tenants among themselves and with respect to the property.

So, is it safe to rent your flat for rooms? In the first place, it must be taken into account that the security of the rent translates into the person with whom you hired, rather than in the contractual modality chosen. We should also know that, in the rental of rooms, we are formalizing several differentiated contracts with different people, and this can generate different pros and cons. Obviously, the legal security of formalizing a lease, as long as all the clauses are specified, will allow us judicial assistance in case of default. It is true that when this contract is governed by the civil code, it gives us the freedom of pacts, and we must not adhere to deadlines or other conditions established by the law of urban leases.

BUYING A CAR OR HOUSE

Buying a car or house? Practically, out of every ten newlyweds, a dozen has this type of doubt, don't you? Making long-term decisions like these is one of the needs of those who come together in marriage. Despite the requirement to have answers ready, those recently married are not always prepared to choose where to invest the money, now managed jointly. Although the couple is aware that it is important to build equity in order to have a better future, they sometimes do not have the total resources necessary to buy all the assets at once, so they need to choose between purchasing a property or a vehicle. Before thinking of buying a car, you need to put some important things into consideration:

Do financial planning

Married life is quite different from single life. In single life, each person could take care of their own money, acquire what they liked best, spend without thinking about the future, among other things. However, after marriage, the finances need to be planned in partnership so that the needs of the whole family are met. Thus, newlyweds should list their usual sources of income and all monthly expenses. Based on this diagnosis, they will be able to carry out efficient financial planning, which should foresee amounts destined for each category of expenditure, such as housing, food, transportation, health and leisure, in addition to savings targets. With this analysis of financial life, the couple will be better prepared to decide whether to buy a car or a house. After all, the diagnosis allows the spouses to identify the couple's ability to pay and, as a consequence, how much they can spend on the acquisition of goods.

Analyze the impact of the asset's value on the household budget

Most of the time, the cost of a property will be higher than the price of a car. As they are durable goods with significant value, couples generally do not have the full amounts for these purchases at once. Therefore, you have to prioritize what you are going to buy first or find alternative ways to meet those needs. At this point in your life as a couple, there is a great risk that the newly formed family will go into chronic indebtedness, especially if they decide to take out a loan to acquire property and vehicle in one go or even one of the assets. As this type of credit, usually offered by banks and finance companies, has a considerable built-in interest rate, it is common for people to pay double or even triple the value of the asset in the total settlement. In the family's day-to-day life, often, an acquisition of this size, when it is financed, becomes a burden on the domestic budget since it compromises a considerable part of the income for several years. Then, the family information is pressured for a long time, which can even compromise coexistence and harmony in the home, due to deprivations.

On the other hand, when the couple opts for more economical forms of acquisition, such as the real estate or car consortium, they use the money efficiently since in this modality, there is no interest collection because it is the participants of the groups themselves who unite to self-finance under the coordination of an administrator. Even if in the consortium the couple does not receive the good immediately, the savings generated by this form of acquisition contribute so that the family does not get into debt; after all, they will not need to give an entry to join the group but only pay the usual installments. If they prefer, the couple can use the money they would give in a group to offer a bid and, with that, anticipate the achievement of the good.

One of the consortium's advantages is that the recipient receives a letter of credit, which allows for a spot deal. In this way, the couple will have greater bargaining power to ask for a discount when buying a car or home.

In case you want to make a somewhat difficult decision of buying a home or a car, you need to consider what you want as a couple. Does the family immediately want to have a child, or do the newlyweds prefer to stabilize themselves and invest in their careers first? The answer to that question will provide an important foundation in the decision to buy a car or home. If the couple prioritizes, initially, perfecting professional training and seeking a better placement in the job market, it may be useful to purchase a car first to facilitate commuting and leave the purchase of a house for later.

Thus, because they are not bound to a territory, the couple may feel more comfortable to eventually change cities in a possible job offer. For that reason, the rent may be bearable if the couple wants to be ready for a sudden change. In another situation, if the priority is to have a child, it is better to have the security of a home of their own so that the child can develop, and the family is able to raise the baby with ease. In this case, rent could represent a certain vulnerability, especially if the economy is not doing well, and there is a chance of a drop in income. Whatever the option of the newlyweds, it is recommended to first prepare the future situation before leaving the current reality so that this transition is the least costly in financial terms.

For example, if both works, one may be responsible for paying the rent and the other for the consortium portion. Thus, the family avoids excessive interest on financing and does not fail to have a home for the initial years of living together. In the case of commuting, it may be useful to use public transport or application services to save money and schedule the purchase of the car itself when there is more financial freedom. As you can see, there is no single recipe for newlyweds when it comes to buying a car or home. Thus, the goals and reality of each couple will define the best choice.

RETIREMENT PLAN FOR COUPLES

Planning retirement as a couple is almost an obligation for those who plan to share their lives. However, we do not always face it correctly. And, in fact, finance is one of those issues that is perhaps least faced when it comes to forming a couple. Something that, of course, is not a good idea. Learn to talk together about personal finance before planning retirement; we must be able to overcome other milestones. The first of them, without a doubt, is to be able to talk openly about personal finances as a couple. And, of course, being able to do joint planning that fits well with personal planning. This goes far beyond agreeing on a common fund or having common objectives in the medium term. It is, first of all, to achieve a broad knowledge of the finances of both. Subsequently, to establish common rules and commitments regarding income and expenses.

For example:

- Short-term objectives related to daily expenses

- Medium-term objectives, such as acquiring a vehicle, paying for a vacation, and so on

- Long-term objectives, such as acquiring a home or jointly preparing for retirement

It is important to get used to talking about money as a couple, but it is also good to order the conduct of domestic finances. For this, a good joint review of the financial products already in place will be necessary. Also, of course, life insurance, savings, or any type of insurance product. Of course, any personal project must also be accommodated here. If trust is one of the foundations of the operation of any relationship, this trust must also occur in the economic aspect. Personal projects do not have to be at odds with common projects. In fact, it is very healthy from both the point of view of the objectives and from the point of view of the investment.

Plan savings and investment

Being able to do all of the above will make it much easier to consider saving and investing. There is no magic book for investment as a couple. In fact, it will probably be different for each couple. When one of the two has more financial knowledge or investors, it is interesting to share this knowledge. The goal is for both of you to feel comfortable and understand what is happening with your money. This is basic. Not understanding what happens with our money is the worst idea when saving or investing. When both partners have similar financial knowledge, the question lies in being able to learn together. This really does not have to be complex. Access to savings and investment products today is much simpler and clearer. In addition, traveling this path as a couple can be rewarding. You learn to value much more than common money, common goals, and, ultimately, the value of proper wealth management.

Save for retirement

Saving for retirement is key for any couple. The approach should be very similar to everything we've seen so far. Clear objectives must be set. How much money are we going to need to not lose our joint purchasing power? This is the question we must ask ourselves when thinking about retirement savings. Personal strategies will also fit here, in addition to joint strategies, but all this must always be agreed and known by both. Depending on the moment and the type of profile of the couple, the financial tools will be different. From savings insurance to direct investment in assets, not forgetting the tax benefits of products such as pension plans, everything can be worth it. It is about understanding what we hire, planning what we allocate to savings and investment, and, ultimately, maintaining a common goal without losing joint participation in the development of that goal.

CHAPTER FOURTEEN
NAVIGATING FINANCES IN A BREAKUP

Despite the sadness and disappointment that the end of a commitment can cause, the moment of separation should be seen as an opportunity to take new steps towards your happiness. One of the first steps you should take during this stage of your life is to organize your finances after separation. Joint accounts, shared expenses, alimony and expenses with the process of dissolving your union must be taken into account in this very delicate moment. By observing some small and important details and organizing finances after separation, you guarantee a little more tranquility in such a troubled time in your life. In order for you to be able to organize finances after separation, it is very important that you have full control of expenses and other charges that may arise during the process and even measures that must be taken to avoid further inconvenience.

Organize finances after separation

To organize finances after separation, you must follow some important steps, such as creating a spending plan.

Bank accounts

Many couples have joint accounts or share credit cards. When organizing finances after separation, it is essential that you keep this in mind and individualize all banking ties. If you and your ex-partner have a joint account, to avoid headaches, cancel the account. This is also true for credit cards. You don't want to have any unpleasant surprises like strange movements of your money or improper purchases in your name, right? Even if your separation is friendly and you trust each other, it is important that, for your own sake, the banking aspects are the first to be reviewed. To start your life over on the right foot, it is essential that you pay attention to this detail.

Expenses with children and alimony

The separation for couples with children is more delicate and needs special care. Even with court orders for the payment of child support and expenses for children, it is important that you keep in mind that your children will also be involved in the process. To organize finances after the separation, you must negotiate with your ex-partner the division of expenses with the children. School, food, entertainment, and every detail of the little ones' lives must be carefully observed so that the division is fair and consistent with the parents' income and so that neither party is financially burdened.

Separation of assets

The separation of assets is always a delicate moment during the breakup of a commitment. However, it is essential for you to be able to organize finances after separation and have a starting point to start your life over. If your relationship was made with the total sharing of assets, you can share everything that was acquired during the relationship. A fair distribution for both and made in a friendly way ensures that even with the end of the union, respect for someone who was very special prevails.

Part 3
FINANCIAL PLANNING WHILE MARRIED

A world's view

The next and one of the best stages of life is at the point whereby the dating couples' transition from being engaged to married. Planning for a good wedding is a very essential and exciting time for many people, which involves budgeting with the use of limited resources, honeymoon and also life after getting married and having a family.[9] Being married brings additional responsibilities that may take the family on debts like to purchase a home or for traveling purposes. When making certain decisions, it is important not to overcommit oneself financially. Therefore, being financially literate will allow married couples to track their spending and budget. Budgeting and tracking a family's spending are essential to financial management and the future of the family. The main aim of tracking a family's spending is not about monitoring the financial expenditures of each family member but to track where the money goes to help set goals that will guide the family to financial security.[10]

Understanding personal finances also help the married couples to set their financial priorities together; like in terms of education for their kids, mortgage and other factors such as vacations.[11] For example, one of the couples might think that

---

[9] Ross, *Money matters in marriage*, 576

[10] Gamst-Klaussen, Thor, Piers Steel, and Frode Svartdal. "Procrastination and personal finances: Exploring the roles of planning and financial self-efficacy." *Frontiers in psychology* 10 (2019): 775.

[11] Ross, *Money matters in marriage*, 578

purchasing a home is more essential, while the other believes that saving for kids' education and retirement is crucial. Therefore, having a good sense of personal finance will help the married couples avoid marital problems and set their priorities right as married people by ensuring that they are on the same page and that they are all working towards a common and mutual financial goal.

Another important aspect is that it will help to offer family security. Providing financial security to a family is one of the most essential aspects of the process of financial planning. Many families always long for financial security, whereby factors such as having appropriate insurance policies and coverage come with peace of mind for all family members. By having good understanding of personal finances, the married couples will know if they can cater to the family's needs whether the country's economy is good or not. Therefore, to have a sense of financial security, married couples need to plan their finances and to be able to plan their finances; they need to have a good understanding of their personal finance education.

Another important aspect is being able to grow assets for the whole family.[12] For any married couples, owning assets is always one of their priorities as it acts as an essential form of a financial cushion. However, research has shown that many assets have attached liabilities, which make it crucial for couples to have adequate knowledge of personal finances and be able to determine their assets' real value.

Another important aspect is that it helps to improve the standards of living for the family. Savings that are often created by being able to plan one's personal finances is highly beneficial

---

[12] Ardi, Ridwan, and Sudarjah. "The use of financial literacy for growing personal finance." 450]

for families especially during difficult moments.[13] For example, by having good knowledge about one's personal finances, they can be able to ensure that insurance coverage is enough to replace any income that is lost especially when one of the married couples loses their main sources of income.

---

[13] Zimbardo, Clements, and Leite. "Time perspective and financial health. 38.

CHAPTER FIFTEEN
PAYING FOR THE WEDDING AND HONEYMOON

Did you find the person of your dreams and decide to marry? So, you need to know that having good financial planning for a wedding is the best way to achieve everything you ever imagined! From home to trips through the most beautiful landscapes in the world, anything is possible, as long as you know what to prioritize and how to carry out each endeavor.

Wedding reception

The wedding reception is usually the first concern of those who decide to get married, isn't it? Guest list, decorations, church, buffet, music, accommodation for those coming from outside, wedding dress, ball: it is a real infinity of details that only the bride and groom decide. The problem is that all of this can cost a lot of money. For these and others, it is simply essential to have financial planning for a wedding. At that moment, you can set a maximum budget for the reception and do a lot of research to get the best prices. Planning in advance can already generate good savings in the months leading up to the big date.

Honeymoon

The second big decision of couples in love usually involves the honeymoon. Usually, the thought runs to imagine a great trip, with paradise-like landscapes, something really unusual. In this regard, it is possible to go from 8 to 80 in the blink of an eye, with budgets from the most modest to the most expensive. And this scenario requires the common sense of the couple not to spend all the savings at once. Considering that the honeymoon is not the highest priority in this phase, it is worth looking for promotional packages, talking to travel agencies or creating your own itinerary. Determining a daily budget for honeymoon spending is also a good way to keep your financial planning for your wedding within limits.

Family car

A car to share or two cars to maintain indepencence? This is also an issue to be considered when doing financial planning for a wedding. In practice, two cars mean double spending on fuel, insurance, licensing, maintenance, and so on. However, we must remember that they are durable goods, serving the owners for a long time. As long as you keep maintenance up to date and take proper care, a car can last for 10 years with peace of mind. In addition, if you want to change your car at some point, this item can serve as a value addition to your letter of credit for the purchase of a more expensive vehicle. It is often preferable to save on the wedding reception and honeymoon, which are fleeting moments, to have a benefit that will affect the whole family for a long time.

Owning a home

Owning a home can be a wonderful experience because you own the place and can do whatever you please, and in a lot of cases it helps you build equity in the property which is as good as having cash. If you want to own a home soon, it is best to invest in financial planning for your wedding right now! We can already say that the dream of owning a property can be achieved in several ways, with cash and financing being the most sought-after options. If you have time to wait, the cash option is definitely the best option since there is no interest to be paid, but not everyone can buy real estate with cash. If you cannot buy a property with cash, there's always the option to get a mortgage as leverage to own the house of your dreams. Are you about to get married and do not want to worry about rent? Do you want to be able to renovate the house to make it your own and still build equity and value over time? Well, speak with a licensed real estate agent to help you reach your goal of becoming a homeowner.

Arrival of children

How many couples forget to plan the arrival of the heirs and then see there was no money left for the preparations? No one dares to doubt the fact that having children is a huge responsibility. Knowing this, being prepared for this life change is simply essential. Saving or investing in an account that earns interest until the couple is officially pregnant can save serious headaches, you know. After all, when we have the resources to meet needs like these, everything flows smoothly. On the other hand, if the change is not expected, we end up frustrated and lose the best part: the expectation of the arrival of the children.

Security application

The couple's life can be shaken by the resignation of one of the spouses, the lack of money to honor the commitments made or even by a health crisis, for example. Taking this type of situation into account is that when making the financial planning for a wedding, you should think about an emergency expenses, an application that stays there, theoretically forgotten, only making a profit while there is no problem. In this context, when a barrier appears, there is no need to worry, as you will be supported to face any financial difficulties. When you're young, thinking about this type of event can seem a little contradictory. However, the fact is that we are all subject to life's unforeseen events, and the one who is ready to face any situation is better off.

Concern about retirement

As much as this may seem like a distant scene now, the truth is that eventually, the moment will come when you will want to stop working to enjoy life a little more. Thus, being prepared for that day is also essential, and it should be a choice of the couple since the beginning of their life together. Making a private pension, 401k, investment properties and other passive income options are some great ways to start planning your retirement now. Leaving the hustle and bustle of the city and spending the weekends in a quieter place or actually moving after retirement are dreams that many people have in their heads, so the better you're prepared the more you'll enjoy your retirement. Remember retirement is not about age, but about preparedness. If you're fully prepared you can retire in your 30's or 40's. Find out more ways to retire early at www.madbu.com under the "retirement" category.

How to make the wedding budget simple?

A simple wedding budget is easy to do. It is everything you need to organize a wedding reception with little money and financial awareness. The worst part of organizing a wedding is the budget. Planning and finding out how much you can spend, in addition to being exhausting, brings out the reality of your pocket. And there's no use running away, every social class needs a complete and well-planned budget. Start with talking it out with your partner about the things you both want to see in the wedding, then start searching the price of these options. Also, you should already have an idea of how much you want to spend on this wedding, so every option chosen should fall within your budget. Do not increase your budget to accommodate more options but decrease your options to fit within your budget.

And that's when the thing starts to get complicated.

The first step in making a wedding budget is to be down to earth and face reality with maturity! Things are not always the way we imagine, and there is no point in wanting a $50,000 wedding if you only have $10,000! At first, it may hurt, but you will find that knowing the real amount you can spend will make it easier.

Who is paying for the wedding?

Talk to your family and have the groom talk to his family to find out who will pay what, whether the bride's family will pay most, or, in most cases, the bride and groom will pay most of the costs. The ideal is to talk to each family separately, so you will have more freedom to discuss, the bride only with her family and the groom with his. After talking to everyone and knowing how much each person will "donate" to the reception, just add all the contributions, and then you will have your budget! Of course, this can change over time; it may increase or decrease, so always be careful and cautious in your decisions. If your family members are paying for the reception, you can choose split responsibilities. Parents help with the house, and the bride and groom pay for the reception; the bride's parents pay for the reception, and the groom's parents pay for the ceremony; each one helps as they can and wherever they prefer! That is, don't pressure anyone. Your parents may not have the same income as you or the groom's parents, so be patient. It is very important for the bride to help pay for some things, no matter how much the parents can afford. This gives more value to every penny spent and controls costs.

How much do you really need to pay for the wedding?

Just like buying shoes, an apartment or that dream bag, when it comes to the reception, you must find out how much you will need to spend to have what you have dreamed of your whole life. You might have a dream a wedding in mind, but will the money be enough for the planning time you want? There is no point in searching Google wedding budget for 100 people or 300 people. It varies with your pocket and your lifestyle; receptions for 80 people can cost more than one for 150 depending on the options and locations. So, don't believe in miracles! Here's a basic summary of what you're going to spend and the percentages for you to work out a controlled spending split:

Reception (buffet, tables and chairs, glasses, dishes, drinks, cake and sweets, etc.): 48%–50%, Ceremony: 2%–3%, Clothing (groom, bride, bridesmaids): 8%–10%, Flowers: 8%–10%, Entertainment/Music: 8%–10%, Photography/Video: 10%–12%, Printed: 2 –3%, Alliances: 2%–3%, Parking/Transportation: 2%–3%, Souvenirs: 2%–3%, Miscellaneous: 8%.

In this budget, there should be about 5% reserve for emergencies; that is, unexpected situations that can happen in an outdoor wedding (rain = tent rental) or your honeymoon, which may be at another time. If you don't plan each expense properly, what was $10,000 becomes $20,000, and before you realize it, you are already in debt! Do not go in debt for your wedding because you don't want your happy moment to turn into a lifetime of debt.

As soon as you and your fiancé(e) hit the hammer and decide the approximate date for the wedding reception, you should start saving as much of your income as possible for the reception, 20% of which would be ideal, although painful. The more time you have to plan the party and save money, the more relaxed the whole process will be. Think about it like this; if I can buy a $200.00 bag or a $300.00 shoe, I can save it for my wedding. Automatically debit your checking account for savings and schedule it right after the day you receive your paycheck. Do this for months before you get married and you will soon realize how much money you spent on nonsense.

Ways to save on your wedding

Limit your spending on small things. Start with small changes that are unlikely to affect your quality of life, but after a year, that extra money will cover some wedding items. Many brides do crazy things, and it's a real drama to get what they want. It is not because the parents are paying for the reception that you have to take everything from the most expensive or just go demanding things and keep crying. Don't spend everything on the ceremony then have no funding to pay for a reception because that is just crazy! Another thing I think is silly is to believe that researching ways to save on the wedding is an indication that your party will be cheap. There is no direct correlation between how much money you spend on a wedding and how much happiness you experience in your newly built family. Weddings can cost $300,000, but I am sure that after one hour, this bill will start to weigh in your pocket, and you will need to make cuts! In short, think that it is not just the reception, there are also new costs of married life that is totally different from living in your parents' house, like rent or a mortgage, utility bills, groceries, insurance, medical bills, and more

How to figure out your wedding budget

Yes, it is difficult to set a budget for your wedding. Whether you are making $100 or $100,000, there are some general guidelines that can help you decide what you can use, save or spend. To begin, the wedding budget planning process is divided into six simple steps.

Step 1: Figure Out Who's Contributing

Perhaps it's just you and your fiancé. Or maybe your parents or other family members want to chip in. Whatever the case may be, finding out who's eager to contribute to your wedding is a good first step in calculating your overall budget. Try to ascertain how much each party is willing to spend, or what particular aspect of the wedding they'd like to take care of. For example, maybe Grandma has her heart set on buying you a wedding dress.

Yes, we realize that money conversations can be super awkward, but knowing who your contributors are is essential to figuring out your bottom line. Just be sure to approach these conversations in a respectful way and be okay with hearing, "Sorry, I'd love to help, but I can't."

Step 2: Crunch the Numbers

Once you have an idea of how much financial assistance you'll receive, focus on your own contribution. How much can you and your fiancé realistically—and comfortably— afford to spend, given all the real-life expenses you have to cover? Based on your monthly income, how much can you both reasonably save between now and the wedding? How much, if any, can you responsibly pull from an existing savings account? Estimate your personal wedding budget based on your answers to the questions above. Then add any other financial contributions that you're confident are coming your way in Step 1.

Step 3: Estimate Your Guest Count

Given an approximate budget, we need an estimated number of guests. Wedding costs are based on the number of guests. The number of guests to attend will determine not only the size of the venue but also the amount of food and alcohol that must be served (this is the two largest of the wedding expenses). Treating your wedding as a "one person" expense can help keep costs in perspective. The guest count generates the number of items to pay, such as invitations, table and chair rentals, cake pies, wedding favors, and more. Being strategic about who you call is a great way to reduce your marriage expenses. Let's start.

Step 4: Pick the Non-negotiable

You and your fiancé might have different opinions about which wedding items are worthwhile. Your fiancé may need an open bar, but you want your guests to avoid getting drunk in favor of spending money on gourmet 5-course meals. In any case, each of you must answer this question: What are the wedding items on your priority list? Once you have determined your top priorities, you can allocate a large portion of your budget to them; this will ensure you have the remnants of other wedding items that are very important to you.

Step 5: Investigate

There are many outstanding hidden costs that need to be considered before your wedding budget falls to the floor. For example, you can't often afford a wedding cake. You need to pay a discount. You don't just pay the rent for the place; installation fees and malfunctions may occur. In addition, there is a total number of suppliers. Do you know where to go with this? No wonder the wedding budget is running low! So, educate about the "hidden" costs. There will be fewer surprises, and results may be closer.

You also need to know the price of the goods at the selected area and station. Obviously, a wedding at a New York hotel or in a park in Tucson, Arizona, will have different costs. The same is true for weddings on a Saturday in June and Wednesday in March. Research the type of wedding you want, be honest about meeting your budget, and adjust your plans accordingly.

Step 6: Do the Math

After completing all five steps above, it's time to do a final reality check: Does your budget breakdown match the actual cost of your ideal wedding? Once your estimated budget and your ideal wedding come pretty close to each other, create a spreadsheet and allocate a certain dollar amount to each aspect of the event. We recommend using Google Sheets so that you can easily share your spreadsheet with your fiancé, parents, and anyone else who is contributing or helping you stay on budget.

Please Don't Go Into Debt to Say "I Do"

Here comes the Public Service Announcement: If you want a harmonious marriage (and who doesn't?), don't start out drowning in debt. Think beyond the "big day" to your "big life" and smarten up. We all know what the #1 cause of divorce is, right? If it is too expensive for your budget, it is possible that you don't need it. And trust us when we say, you can totally have a champagne wedding on a beer budget. You just need to get a bit creative and focus on the feeling of the event rather than the price tag.

Sensible Spending Tip 1: Start putting aside some savings as soon as you get engaged.

Sensible Spending Tip 2: Use your credit cards responsibly. It's tempting to rack up credit card points during wedding planning but try to pay off the balance immediately so that you don't accrue interest!

Sensible Spending Tip 3: Open up a separate wedding checking account, so it's easy to see exactly where the money is going.

And, again, remember that it's not about how much money you spend, it's how much joy you feel. At the end of the day, even if you get married for $50 in a courtroom in a simple white dress (or suit!), it will still be an incredibly beautiful and meaningful wedding. Plus, you'll be able to afford that cab ride home. Win–win!

BUDGETING FOR THE HONEYMOON

How much money to allocate to organize the honeymoon?

Couples should book between 10% and 15% of their wedding budget for their honeymoon. Approximately 15% of the amount of money we plan to spend on the entire wedding should be set aside to organize the honeymoon. For example, if we have the idea of spending about $20,000 in general, the honeymoon should allocate $3,000. However, the tendency is to go to higher quantities, and sometimes, certain economic difficulties are generated. In this line, honeymoon costs are often overlooked while couples organize their wedding. What can we consider spending when drawing up a specific plan? Can we organize it in some way?

Steps to follow

If the couple is going to pay the celebration for themselves, the ideal is that they have practically 100% of the total cost of the wedding, although later, they will recover part of it with gifts from the guests. However, the latter may not respond to the level they expected, which could present in a problem. If it finally comes out positive because they recover their savings or, in many cases, they use it for the honeymoon, it is recommended that each couple manage a budget appropriate to their possibilities and plan the honeymoon with time to save the time it takes. That way, there will be no problems organizing a wedding trip that moves around realistic numbers. In addition, choosing dates outside the strong holiday seasons can be of great help. Opting for more modest accommodations or organizing the trip on your own can also be an alternative. Today, there are many options to reduce travel expenses without giving up a distant destination or certain luxuries.

Ideas to raise money for the wedding:

1. Organize "garage sales"

This is great for clearing the house or office of objects that we no longer use and take away space. Many of us have pairs of shoes we only use once, and this is the time to earn extra money and connect with the neighbors.

2. Sell online

If you are not very sociable or yours are not face-to-face sales, try it online. Market and auction sites are an excellent way to sell old items, collections, and, of course, also new things.

3. Sales by catalog

If you trust any product, do not hesitate to promote and sell it on your own. Selling is a very useful skill and can leave you with a lot of profit.

4. Sale of homemade desserts

If you make great desserts and cakes, this is the time to sell them to people other than your close relatives. In addition to having fun, you will realize the profit that comes from these desserts.

5. Do you know another language?

Give Skype private lessons to people who need to learn but are too busy to go to classrooms personally.

6. Sell unusual things

Sound effects, photos, voice services, recipe creation, wardrobe organization, anything you're good for! And above all, never give up, these are just some of the many ways to generate income.

CHAPTER SIXTEEN
REVISE THE BUDGET

Those are not single words. 82% of engaged or newly married couples say they feel closer when they agree on economic issues, 37% of couples admitted that they talk about their finances every month. If you do not, it would be advisable to schedule a talk about money. I am a firm believer in the 'financial summits' of couples, especially when they begin to live together or get engaged because, at that time, their lives begin to merge. If a couple begins to live together, they must address issues of daily life, such as creating a budget and setting financial responsibilities. You have to set financial goals and decide how much you can borrow, how much to save to buy a home, plan for the future, including retirement, vacations and the arrival of children. The first talk of this kind can be boring since you have to address many issues and maybe reveal some things that were saved. But when they take your hand, conversations are easier.

Some recommendations for these talks:

- Program it

Do not take your partner by surprise by raising an important economic issue. Schedule a talk, so you are both mentally prepared. These talks should last hours. If differences arise on a specific topic, give yourself time to analyze things. After one of these conversations, a person may feel the need to deal with certain feelings, so make sure you have time to think about it or to talk about it with your partner.

- Prepare an agenda

If the talk is structured, things will be easier.

Start with the things that are going well. Did they stick to the budget or save what they set out? Celebrate it! Consider new issues that may have arisen. Do you want a puppy? Do you need a new car? Do you have to pay a large bill for medical treatment? This is the time to solve that. Talk openly and honestly about the obstacles that complicate the achievement of the objectives: long-term plans– the goals for the future and what needs to be done to achieve them.

Do not exceed the set time. It is better to postpone any decision than to keep talking for hours, getting tired and getting more frustrated. You won't solve everything in the first talk, the third or maybe the tenth, so write the remaining issues and address them in future talks. In each conversation, plan what you are going to do around these issues.

- Create a suitable climate

Turn off phones and the television. Play music Pour yourself a drink. Sit close to each other and start talking. You have to generate good waves, and when you're sitting close, it is as if the two of you are working together to solve something and not face each other. Be honest, and don't judge the other. Be careful when tensions arise. If the environment warms up, take a break. Admit that there are tensions, relax, take a break and resume the talk. If the conversation turns negative, pause, and resume later. Remember that the most important thing is the relationship and that you are in this together.

One of the financial strategies that many couples use is to divide expenses together to save money. However, dividing the expenses many times is not as easy as it seems since the couple can have other financial commitments, such as debts, paying maintenance, or their buying habits are simply very different.

To avoid tensions and misunderstandings, here's how you can divide expenses effectively:

Make a budget

It is important that you have a conversation about your personal finances and budget together. In this way, you will be able to know what the state of your finances is, how much money you have available and what your financial goals are. It is recommended that you have this conversation as soon as possible to determine which expenses should be shared and which not.

Establish how expenses will be divided

The most popular strategy is to divide expenses together, and everyone is responsible for their personal experses, such as paying for their phone, car, clothing and personal tems.

However, some couples who do not have the same income decide to divide their expenses in common by contributing a percentage of their income, as if each one contributes the same amount of money, one of them may not be able to cover his personal expenses. Therefore, whoever earns the highest income will pay more, but both will contribute the same percentage of their income. For example, if Vanessa and Paul decide to contribute 20% of their income to cover common expenses, but Vanessa earns $1,500 and Paul $1,000 per month, Vanessa will contribute $300 and Paul $200 to cover common expenses. Likewise, other couples decide to choose what common expenses each one will pay. For example, one person is responsible for paying the costs of electricity and the other person for water costs. However, you should be very careful when dividing expenses in this way since it is advisable to divide the expenses fairly and without affecting the personal finances of the other person.

– Determine if you will open a joint or separate bank account

If you decide that the common expenses will be divided in half, you can open a joint bank account to deposit the money that will be used to pay the shared expenses. Each will contribute the agreed amount to the account from their personal or individual account.

Setting a long-term financial plan

Money is something that always generates many problems for couples who are not very clear. It is important that in the long-term, the couple's finances are organized since this can trigger stress and cause serious problems in the relationship and the family. Whatever financial goal a couple set out, whether it be the acquisition of a mortgage and automobile loan or an investment, it is important that the couple communicate and agree to establish common goals. It is important that long-term goals are set as a couple and not just day-to-day issues. Most of the financial problems stem from complications in communication and not knowing the goals that each one has. It is important to reach an agreement and establish joint objectives. The vast majority of couples are looking to have long-term peace of mind that allows them to have a standard of living outside financial stress. The problem is that everyone wants that, but nobody does anything to reach this goal. Another problem in not having a financial plan as a couple is that you don't work as a team to obtain benefits, which causes fights and conflicts. It is recommended that couples sit down to discuss what they want and what they are looking for and establish a plan on how to reach that goal. Couples who have defined their vision and long-term goals, if they have that confidence or that transparency, have the peace of mind of having a common fund. Another tool is to propose a spending limit to avoid debt and make a budget. Subsequently, you should review how the expenses will be distributed. Have a three-step financial plan. The first is to accumulate savings for terms of three months to one year; the second is to look for investment where there can be attractive profits; and the third is to have a savings fund in case of a contingency, crisis or eventuality.

In some situations, your partner might be in doubt about a joint financial relationship, so you can implement a four-step idea to build trust as the relationship proceeds.

- Splitting expenses

- Set a regular budget meeting

- Taxes for the married couple

- Setting a long-term financial plan

CHAPTER SEVENTEEN
ESTATE PLANNING

Many couples want at least some time to relax after the excitement and intensity of a honeymoon or wedding day. While this break is certainly welcomed, a newly wedded couple will not miss out on the business details that occur immediately after the wedding day.

Change of name

If one or both spouses change their last name, it is important to resolve this issue and inform everyone who knows the previous name. For the change to be legal, the name change spouse must notify the Social Security Service before a new Social Security card is issued. The Social Security office needs a copy of the marriage license and a specific form that can be found on its website. Next, you will need a new driver's license. Usually, you need to go to the department of motor vehicle with your marriage license and your current driving license. You will have to pay fees to issue the new license. You also need to change your passport. You can do this by mail, send your current passport, copy of your marriage license, the required forms, fees and photos. I'm happy to start using the new name, but it's important to remember that it may take some time to change your government ID, such as your passport or driver's license. So, if you plan to travel soon after the wedding, you should register with your current name so that you will not have any problems with providing your ID. In addition, your employer must be notified of your name change so that your benefits remain in your official name. If you want to change your email address, business card or stationery, notify your employer before the wedding.

Combined assets

Whether to change the name or not to change it. You and your spouse may decide to convert part or all of your financial accounts into a joint account. You can change your bank account by going to your local branch and providing the relevant ID. If you have a brokerage or investment account, we suggest you contact your financial advisor to indicate this purpose.

Changes in beneficiaries

If you do not register your spouse as a beneficiary of life insurance, you should consider whether to make this change. If your spouse adds your name after the marriage, check that your name is up to date on your insurance information in case your old last name is showing instead of your new last name.

Notice to the insurance company

Often, one or both spouses have multiple insurance contracts in the event of a mishap. When couples get married, it may be cheaper to use joint policies than separate policies. The deadline for changing the amount of insurance varies.

Therefore, you should consult your employer's HR department or insurance agent to ensure that you do not miss the opportunity to add your spouse to your coverage. For example, if both spouses have health insurance through their employer, obtaining family insurance through an employer may be cheaper. However, adding a spouse to your coverage requires a short period of 30 days from the date of the wedding. If you do not meet the deadline, you may lose control of the business details involved. Be careful when two people become a legally married couple; it is important to address these details so that your marriage begins smoothly.

Will

If you are a new couple, you may not think about making a will, but unfortunately, if an accident occurs, or any situation that has prepared our destiny and the document does not exist, there will be a fight for your family to inherit any of your assets left behind. Of course, the issue is much more complicated if there are young children in the family, so don't just think about it, have all the necessary information and get ready to make the will. When there is no will, the State recognizes to inherit the so-called forced heirs, and children are entitled to inherit a third of the deceased's estate, called legitimate. First of all, they are natural or adopted children and married or out of wedlock, and they have all the same rights. The ascendants – the parents, if they are alive, inherit equally. The spouse – the husband or wife, but if they are not legally married, they do not inherit.

There are other circumstances, such as:

- The will can't be found or was destroyed

- If the will was canceled

- It is not indicated who the heirs are, or they died before the testator

- The heir renounces the inheritance

- When the will does not include all heirs

Therefore, it is best to go to a notary and ask for all the necessary information, and, in particular, each case has the solution indicated if they are a couple or if they have children.

Trust

The trust consists of giving the inheritance to some heirs who may or may not dispose of it as they are authorized to do so, in order to finally pass it to other heirs, with no possibility of being lost to other people. It is the way to protect an estate for two generations of heirs, preventing them from disposing of the assets of the inheritance. The person making the trust (trustor or grantor) designates another person (trustee) to keep the estate and transmit it to a third party (beneficiary) in its entirety or part of it. In some cases, the trustor, beneficiary and trustee can be the same person.

The assignment may simply consist of sending the inheritance to the trustee, without the trustee being able to dispose of it. For example, John makes a will appointing his son James fiduciary of his inheritance, with the task of giving it to his grandson Judah when he is of legal age, without James being able to dispose of the inheritance. In this case, Judah will be the one who must pay the tax when James dies, and Judah will only pay if he were a beneficial owner of the inheritance in the event that the assignment as a trustee allows him to enjoy the income, paying the inheritance tax as usufructuary, and the trustee must pay for the rest of the inheritance when he receives it. It is an interesting figure if what is intended is that the estate is maintained for certain relatives.

Update the estate plan

Many see marriage as the beginning of a new chapter, which goes hand in hand with future planning. Amid the hustle and bustle of the newlyweds' lives, it is easy to avoid wondering what would happen if you or your spouse died. It may be an awkward discussion but facing this question head-on will not leave room for uncertainty. In addition, as you acquire assets, such as vehicles, real estate, or precious assets, you can update your will and/or existing revocable trusts that you deem necessary. Joint estate planning can be a viable option for married couples. Depending on the particular situation of a couple, a joint estate plan has possible benefits and disadvantages. If each partner has very different wishes for the distribution of their assets, they can be better served by forming separate estate plans. It is very important to update all your valuable documents after marriage to help strengthen your relationship with your partner and avoid a chaos that can arise when one of you is no longer in the picture.

Power of attorney and Guardianship

Power of Attorney

A power of attorney (POA) is a document that allows one person to act in the place of another individual. Therefore, its core function is for an individual (principal) to designate another person (the agent) to make important decisions on their behalf. The agent can either be granted broad power of attorney or very narrow/limited power of attorney. The broad POA allows the agent to make any personal and financial decisions on behalf of the agent[14]. Limited POA, on the other hand, allows the agent to make decisions in one specific area specified by the POA document. E.g., the document can stipulate that the agent has medical power of attorney or financial power of attorney, which means that they can only make decisions in these two areas. When there is no specific limitation, the POA is said to be a general power of attorney and doesn't need to list the various issues that may or may not be done. However, the person giving up their power to make decisions should have the legal capacity when signing the document and understand what they are doing i.e., they should be mentally competent.[15] However, the agent should also be capable of acting as a POA, or else the power can be transferred to the guardian.

It is recommended that people use the durable power of attorney, which allows the agent to act on behalf of the

---

[14] Fatoullah, Ronald A., Elizabeth Forspan, Jeffrey P. Gorak, and Sidney Kess. "The Critical Importance of a Power of Attorney for Incapacitated Individuals." *The CPA Journal* 87, no. 5 (2017): 10-23.

[15] Manns Jr, F. Philip. "Powers of Attorney under the Uniform Power of Attorney Act Including Reference to Virginia Law." *ACTEC LJ* 43 (2017): 149-151.

principal even after losing their competency, which is essentially the importance of an agent. It is important to note that the POA does not give the agent power to do anything they want and at all times, they just act as fiduciary. This means that they are only obligated to act in the principal's best interests.[16] The principal identifies the main powers that they want the agent to have when drafting the document. When there is no proper and clearly drafted POA, the process of making major decisions can be difficult, expensive and more so time-consuming. In case an individual wants decision to be made for them but doesn't create a POA, the court can make the decision, which is referred to as the process of guardianship.

Difference between Power of Attorney and Guardianship

In case it is too late for one to create a POA and the property and financial matters need powers to manage them, there are limited options with the most common option being guardianship. In most cases, it is a family member who will apply to the local court to be appointed as the guardian.[17] Their roles are very similar to that of a power of attorney, but there are some essential differences that should be noted.

One of the differences is that in POA, one is allowed to voluntarily and privately choose the person who will take care of their affairs. The principal is given the opportunity to make decisions on whom, when, where and what should be taken

---

[16] Fatoullah, (2017)

[17] Sufian, Beth, James Passamano, and Amy Sopchak. "Legal Issues: Guardianship and Supportive Decision Making." In *Health Care Transition*, pp. 293–299. Springer, Cham, 2018.

care of and how it should be done.[18] This means that the principal is the boss of his/her own life and assets. On the other hand, in guardianship, it is the court that determines the most suitable person and the ward is not given any right to decide their future. Unlike in POA, where the principal is the boss, in guardianship, the wards are bossed by the person appointed by the court.

Another difference is based on timing. In a power of attorney, the POA is signed by the principal when they are able or have the capacity while in guardianship, application is only made after the individual loses his/her legal capacity and doesn't have a POA in place.[19]

Cost is also a differentiating factor. Drafting of Power of Attorney is less expensive compared to guardianship. Financial guardians may also require a type of remuneration that can be fixed by the office of the public guardian and, hence increasing the cost.

In a power of attorney, the duration is usually indefinite as the POA stays in place until the granter dies or revoked.[20] On the other hand, in guardianship, a guardian is appointed by the court for a specified amount of time.

In some states, there exists monitoring programs to monitor the guardians while in POA, the agents are not monitored. Also,

---

[18] Manns Jr, F. Philip. "Powers of Attorney under the Uniform Power of Attorney Act Including Reference to Virginia Law." *ACTEC LJ* 43 (2017): 149–151.

[19] Shea, Sheila E., and Carol Pressman. "Guardianship: A Civil Rights Perspective." *A Joint Issue: Guardianship and Surrogate Decision-Making* (2018): 51–56.

[20] Manns

some guardians require minor training while in power of attorney, there is no form of training. Hence, one must trust the qualifications and integrity of the agent.[21]

Given that getting a guardian appointed is highly expensive for many people, unpredictable, linked to a lot of delays and inconveniencies, it is recommended that one takes their time in selecting a power of attorney. This is important as it gives an individual peace of mind and also gives the family an easier time in case one loses their capacity.

---

[21] Sufian

CHAPTER EIGHTEEN
PLANNING FOR THE FUTURE AS A RETIRED COUPLE

Planning retirement as a couple is almost an obligation for those who plan to share their lives. However, we do not always face it correctly. And, in fact, finance is one of those issues that perhaps are faced least when it comes to forming a couple–something that, of course, is not a good idea.

Learn together to talk about personal finance

Before planning retirement, we must be able to overcome other milestones. The first of them, without a doubt, is to be able to talk openly about personal finances as a couple. And, of course, being able to do joint planning that fits well with personal planning. This goes far beyond agreeing on a common fund or having common objectives in the medium term. It is, first of all, to achieve a broad knowledge of the finances of both. Subsequently, to establish common rules and commitments regarding income and expenses. And finally, to set goals in all-time planes.

- Short-term objectives related to daily expenses

- Medium-term objectives, such as acquiring a vehicle, paying for a vacation, and so on

- Long-term objectives, such as acquiring a home or jointly preparing for retirement

It is important to get used to talking about money as a couple, but it is also good to order the conduct of domestic finances. For this, a good joint review of the financial products already in place will be necessary. Also, of course, life insurance, savings, or any type of insurance product. Of course, any personal project must also be accommodated here. If trust is one of the foundations of the operation of any relationship, this trust must also occur in the economic aspect. Personal projects do not have to be at odds with common projects. In fact, it is very healthy from both the point of view of the objectives and from the point of view of the investment.

Plan savings and investment

Being able to do all of the above will make it much easier to consider saving and investing. There is no magic book for investment as a couple. In fact, it will probably be different for each couple. When one of the two has more financial knowledge or investors, it is interesting to share this knowledge. The goal is for both of you to feel comfortable and understand what is happening with your money. This is basic. Not understanding what happens with our money is the worst idea when saving or investing. When both partners have similar financial knowledge, the question lies in being able to learn together. This really does not have to be complex. Access to savings and investment products today is much simpler and clearer. In addition, traveling this path as a couple can be rewarding. You learn to value much more than common money, common goals, and, ultimately, the value of proper wealth management.

Save for retirement

Saving for retirement is key for any couple. The approach should be very similar to everything we've seen so far. Clear objectives must be set. How much money are we going to need to not lose our joint purchasing power? This is the question we must ask ourselves when thinking about retirement savings. Personal strategies will also fit here, in addition to joint strategies, but all this must always be agreed upon and known by both. Time is an important element based on your income, so try to predict how long it will take you to meet up with the necessary fund. The financial tools will be different, depending on the moment and the type of profile of the couple. From savings insurance to direct investment in assets, not forgetting the tax benefits of products, such as pension plans, everything can be worth it. It is about understanding what we have, planning what we allocate to savings and invest, and, ultimately, maintaining a common goal without losing joint participation in the development of that goal. If you work for a company that provides a 401k (403B or similar plan) always participate, and whenever possible maximize your contribution to take advantage of your employer's contribution. The earlier you start planning for retirement the earlier you will be ready to retire. Remember that retirement is about being ready financially and not about reaching a specific age. You can retire in your 30's, 40's if you are prepared, so do not buy into the hype that you have to reach a certain age to retire.

CHAPTER NINETEEN

WHEN TWO BECOME THREE

It is worth mentioning that I do not believe that there is a financially ideal time to have children. It is a greater blessing if children arrive when we have a stable family economy. However, you should not plan your family around your finances. Instead, start practicing good financial habits every day. For example, make a budget every month and record your expenses daily. Plan to save an emergency fund equivalent to six months of expenses. And finally, invest a fixed amount each month for your retirement. If you practice these three habits religiously, you will always enjoy very good financial health. When budgeting to have children, you should consider the different phases of pregnancy, birth, and growth of the baby. And what do you think? Children cost you even when they are not born. The first expenses you will make will be visits to the doctor, medical insurance, and maternity clothes. It is normal for your gynecologist to call you for review once a month. This is an important expense that you should include in your monthly budget. All these expenses can be budgeted in a separate category of "pregnancy." This will help you keep track of how much you are spending on your pregnancy, month by month.

It is definitely essential to budget to have children. The truth is that it is very important for you to make proper financial analysis before having your first child. Babies are blessings that need to be catered for. You need to have a proper budget for the newborn, feeding, clothing, toys, and other accessories before you get pregnant. There are lots of expenses to be catered for during pregnancy, which can affect your saving plans if they are not properly catered for. Prepare a standard savings plan for baby feeding. Babies eat more often than adults. They eat twice, trice, which you never imagined. The baby's health needs proper medical attention that comes with a price tag most of the time, so in order to save your family from impromptu baby needs, create a baby savings plan ahead of the time when you will have your baby.

Use apps/systems that will help you manage your expenses and income better, and if you do not have any system you can go to www.madbumax.com to access a budgeting program to help you stay on top of your finances.

As parents, you have an obligation to ensure that your child has every possible opportunity in their life, no matter what. For this, it is essential, on the one hand, to include their education as a long-term financial objective, and on the other hand, to cover possible catastrophic contingencies through insurance policies.

Their education

Saving for your child's education is investing in the future. There are financial products specially designed for this purpose on the market. A savings-studies plan is a mechanism to establish in the long-term, through periodic contributions of small amounts, capital whose purpose is associated with the children's education, training, or first business needs. In reality, savings-studies can take the form of:

- A safe-saving

- A term deposit

- An investment fund

However, for both the deposit and investment fund modality, optional insurance is usually contracted so that the children charge additional capital to the amount accumulated in the event of the death of the father or mother; this ensures the possibility of continuing to study. The three formulas are supported by a savings book studies in which periodic contributions (monthly, quarterly or annual) are made. They are usually completed with a free professional guidance from a financial advisor. Of course, any product or combination of long-term savings-investment products can serve this purpose. 529 plan is a tax-advantaged plan parents or family members can use to save for a child's future education expenses. Ask your financial advisor about a 529 plan and how you can get started because your child will thank you later.

Insurance

Your emergency fund must cover unforeseen expenses that may arise on a day-to-day basis, such as repairs to your home or car. It also serves to have a safety net in case of a temporary loss of income. However, to protect your family against more momentous events, such as the death or disability of you or your partner, you usually need to take out insurance.

Hands protecting a baby's feet

Life insurance protects your child in case of the death of both parents but also covers your partner against the financial burden of having to raise a child alone. If you already have life insurance, you should review the coverage in advance of your new responsibilities. If only you or your partner is insured, consider the need to ensure both. If either parent dies or becomes incapacitated, the other, even if he had income, would have to face additional expenses in order to take proper care of his child and move forward. Accident insurance is usually cheaper than life insurance and covers the insured with a certain capital in case of temporary or permanent disability or death caused by accident. If you have private health insurance, do not forget to add your child as soon as possible, as waiting periods are normally established. If they have complementary health insurance to Social Security, you will have to add your child as an insured and as a beneficiary. This should be done as soon as possible since most health insurance and private companies establish a waiting period. That is, you must be included for a minimum period of time before you can access certain medical services.

Tips for controlling debts with a baby

When a baby comes into our lives, saving for emergencies is a no-brainer. With the arrival of a baby in the family, there are many habits that need to change–from sleep routines to how to eat, distribution of spaces to financial organization, which includes debts and savings. In order to be able to reshuffle your finances, you will need to appeal to creativity and an organized budget. This way, you can maximize your savings. The family must be prepared for unexpected expenses, which are quite frequent, especially with babies.

The most useful tips to save money when your baby arrives are:

1.- Baby feeding

Maternal breastfeeding is not only the best nutritional option for the baby, but it will also allow you to save a lot of money on formulas, especially during your child's first year of life.

2.- Care for children

One of the biggest expenses in educating a child is nannies or daycare centers. One way to save money is to think about the possibility of a parent working at home. This way, you can be responsible for meeting the needs of the little ones. Not only will there be an economic benefit, but there's also an opportunity to see them grow up close.

3.- Essential purchases

Even if you want to make all the necessary purchases to receive your baby, it is better to wait a while. After the child is born, you will know which bottles, pacifiers, and diapers he/she needs or prefers.

4.- The stroller

Choose a stroller that can fit the baby's size, so it can be used for a longer time. There are also strollers that can turn into beds and chairs, which, in the long run, will help you save money when the baby arrives.

5.- Prices in different stores

Before letting yourself be dazzled by a product, compare the prices of brands and references in other stores. Also, use the

Internet. You can find great deals on the products you need. Saving is not just saving but knowing how to spend.

6.- Food prepared at home

When your baby starts eating solids, avoid buying canned food and prepare the food at home. Cook vegetables and then place them in a food processor with a little liquid to make delicious baby food. It will take a little more time, but the effort will be reflected when you do the math.

7.- Creativity in organization and decoration

Take time to do-it-yourself projects. There are hundreds of options for decorating children's rooms, making toys, and cooking food. In addition, involving your children in these manual activities will be a good excuse to entertain them. With economic and simple elements, you can get real works of art.

8.- Choose wisely what you are going to buy

Although it seems basic, this is one of the tips to save money that is more difficult to apply in everyday life. Even if you are tempted to buy everything you see in children's stores, think about whether you really need it. Sometimes, the thrill of being a parent prevents us from thinking clearly. Children grow up so fast that, in general, they don't get to use everything we buy.

Avoid accumulating and make your purchases in moderation.

9.- Frequent medical exams

An excellent way to take care of your health and prevent expenses with medical care is health examinations. Keep the baby's health under control and that of the whole family to reduce the risk of any disease.

10. – Conservation of objects for future children

If you plan to have more children in the future, a good way to save is to keep things in good condition. If you endeavor to care for and teach care for personal effects, you will have a good reserve for your future children.

11.– Durable objects

If you are going to invest your money buying items for you and your family, make sure they are of the best quality. A durable product will prevent further expenses in the future. Buying unisex objects is also a wildcard to save.

12.– Use of coupons

Many magazines and newspapers give discount coupons on products we use daily. Take advantage of offers and low demand seasons to get the best prices on baby items.

CHAPTER TWENTY
DIVORCE

A world's view

It is not uncommon to see "happily married couples" divorce, given that they are not often likely to spend their lives together. Research shows that the divorce rate around the world, especially in the US, has continued to increase.[22] In this case, research has shown that people reaching their retirement ages may find it hard to solidify themselves financially, especially if they lack appropriate knowledge about personal finances and it is the other partner who was mainly responsible for finances. Research by the AICPA has shown that out of every older people who divorce, three of them lack better understanding of personal finances.

When one has good knowledge about their personal finances, they are able to reorganize and reassess themselves after a divorce, and hence won't be negatively affected. One of the advantages is that it will ensure that you are able to meet your money needs, especially when they don't have a stable income or have retired.[23] Being uninformed on personal finances will have dire consequences in case of a divorce. As it can also make

---

[22] Ross, *Money matters in marriage*, 578

[23] Banthia, Dhananjay, and Mangaraj. "ALiterature Review on Financial Literacy. 100

it easy for the financially sophisticated partner to hide assets or even offer you a bad deal. On the other hand, financial literacy on personal finances enables one to start establishing the foundation for a new and financially independent life ahead. Research has shown that dividing assets can be a challenging process for many couples and divorce means calculating child support and also making sense of investment.[24] Therefore, until one understands their personal finances, they cannot accurately plan for their future after the divorce.

Understanding personal finances have also been found to assist divorced spouses in seeking out financial advice and increase their saving towards retirement. For example, some people are left with huge debts, especially in cases where one of the partners was helping to pay the debt. Therefore, skills in personal finances help one to understand how much they have, earn, their expenses and assist them to budget within means they can afford and be able to pay the debt.[25]

Personal finance skills will also help to increase the cash flow of an individual after the divorce, which might have resulted in the loss of an essential source of income or helper. It helps by monitoring how one spends and nature of their expenses e.g., in legal battles and purchasing property.[26] Therefore, personal finance skills and planning would help one to keep more hard-

---

[24] Ross, *Money matters in marriage*, 577

[25] Gamst-Klaussen, Thor, Piers Steel, and Frode Svartdal. "Procrastination and personal finances: Exploring the roles of planning and financial self-efficacy." *Frontiers in psychology* 10 (2019): 775.

[26] Ardi, Ridwan, and Sudarjah. "The use of financial literacy for growing personal finance." 455

earned cash and also make investments on some of the money or assets they might have gained after divorce.

Personal finance knowledge may also help a divorcee in case of an emergency, given that there are always unavoidable and unexpected circumstances that can become obstacles for them to regain financial stability.[27] Therefore, personal finance skills and proper planning allows an individual always to be ready for such situations.

Effects of divorce

Separation affects both parents and kids. The loss of shared life and the need to abandon future ideas together for families is often a pain. Most people can adapt to the new condition, but if they can't see how the situation progresses, they can go a long way. For a while-sometimes over the years- you reed to provide a grant to you and your child. However, before providing support to your children, it is important to know that you need to feel supported.

What children need to know

You don't have to tell your child all the details about the split with your partner, but it's important that (s)he knows the facts about his future. For example, when can you see ycur father (or mother) and grandparents, uncles, aunts, cousins, and whether they change homes or schools.

How kids express their feelings

---

[27] Banthia, Dhananjay, and Mangaraj. "A Literature Review on Financial Literacy. 101

Children, like adults, respond independently to stress and misery. Their response also depends on age:

Before 5: Young children often feel anxious when away from their parents. This anxiety usually manifests as crying, anxiety, and difficult behavior. The additional stress of disbanding a family is likely to make it more difficult for children to separate and cope with change. (S)he is very reluctant to leave you when the father (or mother) visits and has a tantrum when you say goodbye and go home. This is stressful for everyone, but in some circumstances, it is natural.

6 to 11 years: During the next years of childhood, children already have a better understanding of what is happening, but they still cannot cope with the allegiance of separation associated with separation. They feel responsible for the problem and can even feel guilty. They accept that you understand that they are experiencing that difficult time, and they need to externalize it to the people around them before they can regain their stability. Schools can be a safe haven for children, but if you can't handle friends or the school itself, you need to be patient.

–Adolescence: This is an important time for young people to discover their feelings and identity. For teens, leaving parents can be anxious the moment they begin to lose connection with their families, as part of normal development. Teenagers also feel guilty because they think they have caused the dissolution. Some teenagers address this by showing a desperate attraction to independence as a way to not face what is actually happening at home. For others, uncertainty can make them get closer to the family. It is important for teenagers to stay in touch with parents of the same sex.

Children who show little emotions can be experiencing emotional trauma resulting from the separation. Do not ignore them. Or act like everything is okay. If you are not sure of the type of concern this type of children is experiencing, it may be helpful to consult their teacher, doctor, or health care provider to find out if other outside help is needed.

Children worry about separation and may experience with different coping strategies. As a result, discipline can be a more difficult problem to deal with than before. When your child is with your ex-partner, you may worry about whether your child is free, or you may notice that your new partner is using a different form of discipline from what you are using.

New family

When families are separated, usually, new families are created. With a new partner you may want to create a new future with your new family. It is important to remember that you ask a lot of children when they're trying to cope with the loss of their parents. They need:

- An adult learns to deal with a new adult, and he seems to respond from mom or dad

- Meet new grandparents, brothers and sisters and children born from a new relationship

- Discriminate against the old faith and old feelings

- Act differently, for example, share a bedroom with others or build a new house.

It is important to make sure that even small children do not automatically need new fathers and mothers. Such closeness develops over time, only if a new father (or new mother) and a new child develop this feeling for each other. At the same time, a certain distance is inevitable, and it is better to accept respect for all participants. I do not want your former partner to feel that someone else is dad or mom on your behalf. Slowing down allows everyone to take sensible action.

Spousal support

Your happiness is, without a doubt, above any loss of money. But you can't ignore that going through a divorce has a price that is not only emotional but also financial. You are likely to face some life changes that involve money: a drop-in family income, moving to a new house, and division of assets, in addition to the cost of the divorce itself. But don't stop separating because of money. It's not worth it. With the following tips, this whole process can be less painful for you and your pocket.

1. Know that your lifestyle will change – and prepare for it

The same wages as two people who supported only one house will now maintain two houses – and two lives. You are likely to be forced to reduce your standards of living, at least in the first few months after separation, until you are stabilized. For this reason, do everything you can to reduce the fixed costs to the maximum in this phase. It is a new life. As much as it looks like a hurricane at first, you need to be calm to see that it is just a temporary phase. It is necessary to redo the income and expense accounts with the help of applications or spreadsheets. If you think it's best, turn to a financial advisor.

2. Whoever earns more can pay more for their children

Spending on children should not always be divided. Equally, it depends on the condition of each one. It is quite common and accepted by the law that those who have more income bear more expenses. It is important that people have this clarity and that whoever earns less can position themselves not to assume expenses that they are then unable to pay. In addition, having shared custody means equally sharing all responsibilities for decisions involving children, including financial ones, but not necessarily the child's time with each one.

3. Know all the financial transactions

Before separating, it is essential to know how much money the couple has invested and where that money is. It is also important to participate in all important financial decisions. In the separation, those who did not take care of investments so much will need to be aware of everything. Don't let the ex-spouse take care of your finances, take responsibility for yourself.

4. In the beginning, it's better to rent rather than buy a property

The decision on who will live in the couple's home and who will move depends on a negotiation between the two, or the division of assets established by the judge. It can also happen that both partners leave the property, it is sold, and the money is shared. However, at the moment, it is preferable to keep the property, as it can be difficult to sell because of uncertainties about the future of the economy. You can't throw yourself into any offer. One stays in the house, therefore, and the other leaves. The advice for those who leave is to rent a property at first, instead of buying. This is a phase of uncertainty in life, and buying a property, as it is a high-value asset that you will have for a good part of life, requires a cool head and emotional stability. This is not the time to make decisions on the go. Agreements can also be made, for example, for one to stay at the couple's house for a while, and then it is sold, and the money is divided.

5. If the separation is not very friendly, it is better to have two lawyers.

At least one lawyer for the two is essential to make the divorce, either in a notary or through the courts. It is he who will guide all legal procedures and guide the separation of assets. Remember that you will have this cost with the professional's services. If, in the future, the ex-couple disagrees for any reason, their lawyer cannot represent either one or the other. The relationship may be good today, but we don't know about tomorrow.

6. No matter the income of each one, the assets must be divided equally

The couple's entire life was built by the two equally, even if one has a higher income than the other. Both of them only achieved what they have because they were together, no matter if one did not work or if the other earned more. Therefore, if there was no previous prenuptial agreement that established the rules of what would happen to the assets in the event of separation, the law is clear: all assets acquired after marriage must be divided equally. It is common for one of the two to hide a patrimony when sharing assets to escape the egalitarian division. However, the lawyer makes the reservation that by failing to report the existence of a property, in addition to the chances of suffering an action for damages in the future, the ex-spouse can be accused of committing a crime.

In family law, they say that whoever takes the lead wins. If you are in doubt, immediately ask the lawyer for the necessary evidence. The judge may compel the bank to show all the financial transactions of the ex-spouse, for example.

7. Prepare for divorce costs, at the notary or court

What will determine whether the divorce will be made using notarized forms or through the courts is, how easy an agreement can be reached between the ex-couple and the existence of children? Emotionally, it is cheaper to when the divorce is uncontested because it is faster. Divorces, where there is no equity to share, are cheaper because the couple does not own much or because they married with a total separation of assets. When it is necessary to divice the assets, there are expenses with taxes, property registrations, and costs with the courts or a notary.

Taxes for divorcee

Understand your marital status for the purposes of filing:

As a divorced person you may be eligible to file your taxes as the "head of household".

- If you are employed, change your withholdings.

- The alimony for tax purposes: The alimony is not tax-deductible for the person who pays it, and the support paid will only be tax deductible if their divorce was already final in 2020. Similarly, the person receiving the support must declare it on their tax return if the divorce was already final by January 31, 2020, but alimony is not reported as income.

- Analyze your divorce decree to determine who will declare the children as dependents. If your divorce agreement did not specify who declares the children as dependents, then the parent who has the tenancy does so. If tenure is shared, the parent who spends the most days with the child during the fiscal year is the one who declares it as a dependent.

Division of marital assets

As if the divorce itself was not difficult enough, the division of property becomes a headache for many couples going through a divorce. In many cases, these problems have been a disaster from the first divorce conversations, and some couples may easily agree to keep what was theirs before marriage. However, most couples acquire property and other large items during a marriage, which can be difficult to divide during the divorce process. If you are facing a divorce and have questions about the division of marital property, do not hesitate to contact a lawyer experienced in family law.

DIVISION OF THE MARRIAGE ASSETS

Some properties can be difficult to divide, such as a house, association interests, or expensive works of art. In these cases, the valuation of the property must occur, and one of the spouses must pay the other spouse their share of the property. Many couples often omit the valuation of marital property and simply allow one of the spouses to take the house and the other to take the property from the house if the assets are equivalent in value. This is an acceptable option for many couples, but it comes with many losses as well. A lawyer with experience in family law will be able to point you in the right direction to find an experienced appraiser in the division of marital property.

While most properties are easy to divide during the divorce process, other intangible forms of property, such as a commercial interest, can present some problems. If you entered into marriage by owning your own business or commercial interest, and your spouse helped you by supporting this business over the years, your spouse may have a claim that a percentage of the property is owned by the community. In addition, 401k plans and other employee benefit plans are subject to division. The spouse who owns the benefit plan often pays the other spouse their percentage that they would have been entitled to at that time. If you or your spouse attended school or paid student loans during the marriage, the other spouse would be entitled to reimbursement of these expenses. Entrust your marital property to a lawyer.

Tips for financial protection in a divorce:

1. Open your own credit card

It is important to close joint accounts when the divorce begins to avoid future disputes. Another alternative is to get your partner to separate from those they already have, to keep them in your name.

2. Take care of your credit score

The divorce could cause it to fall. Look for factors that may indicate a problem, such as mistakes made by a creditor or a debt that has accumulated in an account that you are not aware of.

3. Avoid making large purchases

Do you want a new washing machine? A car? "By making a purchase during the separation process, you could end up having to divide it once the divorce is over.

4. Don't get sentimental

People overvalue their possessions. They are important to them, and they usually have an inflated idea of how much they are worth. Prevent this from happening to you! Seek professional advice about the real value of the properties to negotiate on a fair market price, rather than for sentimental issues. So, you know although divorce is a complex process, there are many resources to protect your finances. Make them play in your favor!

5. Separate accounts

Always make sure your insurance, bank accounts, and other joint accounts no longer show the name of your former spouse. In most cases you will not be able to remove their names without their permission. The easy way is to remove yourself from such accounts and create your own accounts unless you can convince your former spouse to remove themselves from the accounts.

CONCLUSION

Managing the financial budget is one of the priorities for any individual. Costs are almost inevitable for many people, both for singles and couples. However, it is important to follow a strict budget to achieve a ba ance in your earnings and spending.

Separate essential expenses

The first step for those who need to cut spending is to identify where the money is going. Without this measure, i: is not possible to filter essential expenses from unnecessary ones. It seems simple, but a lot of people struggle with this step.

Essential spending can be classified as essential expenses that are essential for the upbringing of your home, such as, electrical energy (after all, almost everything in the world needs electricity to function). Although essential, these expenditures can be controlled to provide budget savings, as in the case of electricity, where actions can be taken to reduce consumption. Spending on renting a place where you need to rest and keep your family, the Internet, and water are also essential issues, but depending on the situation, they can become flexible spending. Have you ever thought about changing your job location to reduce the expenses on transport or increase your income, for example?

Flexible spending is that spending that may or may not make a difference in your life, and your cut should be seriously considered. Your addictions, such as coffee and tea, can be stopped and invested for either short-term or long-term goals in your life or business. Your smartphone is also a tricky way of excessive spending, and you can instead use cheaper plans (from lesser-known companies) to reduce the cost of service.

Any self-respecting organization always has a financial plan and budget for a year, two, five, or more years. This helps to plan large expenses, collect all incomes together, and analyze the financial condition. Your family is your organization– it doesn't matter whether you are the only one in it with a cat, or you have a large family of 4-5 people. And the preparation of the family budget should be part of your ongoing annual obligation, especially if you plan to invest available funds in investments. Your budget must cover your major possessions: house/apartment, cottage/land, car, etc., all your savings: bank deposits, card balance for the reporting period, all your income: salary, extra part-time, any interest that comes annually from the contribution, dividends if any. And no matter how nice it would be to fill out the first part of the budget, you still have to come to this; Your expenses such as:

- Utility costs

- Payments on your mortgage/loan or rent

- Food costs (what you eat at home)

- Spending on gasoline (or travel by bus and taxi)

- Spending on entertainment and cafes (going to the theater, cinema, cafes, restaurants, food delivery, etc.)

Having outlined everything on paper, you will have a clear picture of what you spend the most money on, and you will also understand whether you have any free funds left at the end of the month that you can put into your financial cushion or investment. It is advisable to first make a calculation for the whole year, writing in the expenses of the large acquisitions that you plan to buy this year. This will help you understand which month is best to save in order to make a larger purchase next at this stage, and you should show your kids, if you have any, so they can understand what it is like to make a budget and its importance. This will help your child understand how to manage their personal savings when they grow up while they learn from possible mistakes that might have occurred in your budgeting.

Then you consider everything from the point of view of one month and try to redraw your expenses so that in the end, you have extra money left at the end of the month. After all, wealth is not how much you earn but how much you managed to save. Now that you have read and implemented the teaching in this book, it is important for you to guide your children through the process and ensure that you guide them through financial responsibility to help them avoid financial struggles as they grow.

BONUS ONE
ART OF COUPONING

A coupon refers to a document or ticket that a customer can redeem to get a financial discount when purchasing a certain product. Couponing has become a very essential promotion tool used by manufacturers and retailers around the world. Each year, customers around the world are exposed to thousands of coupons that offer potential for savings. The coupons are majorly distributed through newspapers, mail, internet, mobile devices, magazines, coupon envelops and directly from the retailer. According to Prices[28] the art of couponing by organizations function as a type of price discrimination given that consumers who are price conscious will spend a lot of time trying to claim the savings. This allows the retailers to give a discount and low price to customers who would shop elsewhere.

According to marketing researchers, one of the main reasons as to why many customers today go for coupons is to help them save money when buying products and services. Research has shown that even though some people tend to use coupon codes moderately, they have reported significant savings in their budgeting.[29] In the beginning, one might not feel like it is

---

[28] Prices, Mirabegron. "Coupons & Savings Tips. GoodRx." (2019): 5-13.

[29] Ahmed, Kazi Afaq, and Zainab Sarwar. "Consumer Willingness to Use Digital Coupons: A Case of Karachi

worth the hustle because the savings are insignificant. Still, over time, consumers state that they realize significant savings and hence are motivated to keep on using the coupons. However, for one to be able to save money by the use of coupons, it is important to employ a number of strategies that have been identified by couponers.

How to get the coupons?

Over the years, many manufacturers and retailers have been using the local Sunday newspapers to give out their promotion coupons and hence this is one of the most common places to find coupons. Therefore, one of the methods of finding a coupon is checking the Sunday newspapers, which have been reported to contain between $50 to $300 worth of savings in the form of coupon inserts.[30] One can also look up on magazines which have also been known to have coupons printed on ad pages. Another approach to getting coupons is by asking the manufacturer by contacting them directly. A spot check of a number of companies shows that they will often send coupons of samples to the customers when you request them or provide feedback.

Joining store loyalty programs is also a good way to find coupons. Enroll in their newsletters and rewards programs of retailers who you frequent most as research has shown that many stores tend to send their returning customers a lot of exclusive coupons.

Market in Pakistan." *International Journal of Experiential Learning & Case Studies* 3, no. 1 (2018): 33–42.

[30] Choudhary, Vidyanand, and Shivendu Shivendu. "Targeted Couponing in Online Auctions." *Information Systems Research* 28, no. 3 (2017): 490–510.

Another way of getting coupons is by looking at the packaging of the products. Many companies are continually putting promotion coupons directly on the products which can come in the form of peelies, hangtags, and also inside the package. When shopping in the grocery store, inspect the items for a peel-off coupon that might be attached to the packaging. However, with the advent of technology, research shows that organizations are continuously adopting new and innovative ways of giving out coupons, which include the use of technology e.g., online coupon codes or promo links.

How to use the coupons?

After obtaining the coupons, it is important to have a well-laid approach to using them in order to benefit from them in terms of savings maximally. According to Choudhary and Shivendu [31] the use of coupons involves clipping, saving and redeeming and hence, only the customers who will put their effort to redeem them will receive the discounts. Therefore, understanding how to use coupons is very essential in increasing the likelihood of increasing savings. Also, one should be familiar with some of the fine print that is used, which will allow one to budget accordingly. To start using coupons, it is recommended that one approaches it with caution because. The following are some of the recommended tips on how to start using coupons:

Keep the coupons organized: The first thing to do is organize the coupons well in a place they can easily be accessed when need be. Some of the places to store coupons include a

---

[31] Choudhary and Shivendu

container, use a price book and develop a filing system where you can organize the coupons by category e.g. grocery.

Find stores that have good deals: Just because you have a coupon doesn't mean you need to use it. Therefore, find deals in stores where they are giving out products on offers and avoid purchasing expensive products just because there is a coupon. Therefore, to get a good deal, it is important to determine the most appropriate timing to redeem your coupon. E.g. when there is a sale on or a time for seasonal good. Also, it is important to be aware of the savings programs of the local stores before visiting the stores.

Match up the coupons with sales for bigger savings. Coupons matchup is described as the process of matching up one's coupons to the products that are being sold to maximize the savings. To get big returns, one should couple the coupons with sales. It is also essential to buy enough products when they are at low price. This means that one needs to wait for the price of the products to be discounted before making purchases and them buy in bulk.

Shop strategically and avoid buying things you don't need: Research shows that price discounts and coupons drive impulse purchases and this is the reason why many online shoppers buy more impulse compared to offline shoppers. To get the best value out of the coupons, it is essential to avoid impulse buying and plan well what should be bought, and this should help achieve best savings. Additionally, if you get an opportunity to purchase a lot of non-perishable goods at the best price, this has the potential to save you a lot of money.

Potential for saving money

Research shows that different people will use coupons for different purposes. For example, for some people, couponing is their way of life and is an easy approach to save money on bills and invest the money elsewhere. For other people, it is a good way to save a dollar on something they wanted to buy. However, there have been a lot of misconceptions about use of coupons whereby many some researchers argue that this is psychological promotion approach used by organizations to benefit themselves while others have argued that the benefit is mutual as both parties can benefit. However, it can also be argued that with effective couponing and good strategies, one has the potential to realize a lot of savings in their budgets. When used effectively, couponing has the potential of shaving more than 50% off your budget[32]. Regardless of the needs of the family, every family can save on something they buy by use of coupons.

According to a report by ValPak Readership Survey[33], an average household in the United States can save more than $10,000 annually when they use couponing, but also, many people tend to underestimate the long-term effect of couponing on their budget. From the ValPak survey, no single respondents were aware that the use of coupons could save them that much annually, which shows that there is a need for

---

[32] Ahmed, Kazi Afaq, and Zainab Sarwar. "Consumer Willingness to Use Digital Coupons: A Case of Karachi Market in Pakistan." *International Journal of Experiential Learning & Case Studies* 3, no. 1 (2018): 33–42.

[33] Valpak's 2019 coupon engagement survey. www.valpak.com/coupons/home

awareness. As noted by Labor statistics, average families in the United States have annual revenues of about $41,600 and the annual raise is averaged at $1,248. This shows that even by casually using coupons, the savings could be even higher than the average annual pay rise and hence many people still refuse to use coupons. Therefore, couponing has a great potential for saving money. The long-term benefit of using coupons is to save money and many people have reported that they experience experiential or emotional benefit such as happiness and satisfaction.

Tools to help with getting better at couponing

Various people who use coupons have listed some of the tools that have helped them get better at couponing. Some of the tools include a printer, coupon folder, coupon binder, scissors, and paper trimmer.

Coupon folder: This is important for organizing the coupons, especially for new people using coupons. There are different methods of organizing coupons and hence the best method will always depend on the goals of an individual. For example, one recommended method is using a coupon binder or coupon wallet.

Scissors: Scissors are important for clipping the coupons. Different people use different types of scissors, but it is recommended that one invests in good quality scissors while others also use paper trimmers. Paper trimmers have the ability to clip tons of coupons ones which saves a lot of time.

Printer: A printer is an essential tool that the couponer can use to print different kinds of coupons. If one is planning to invest a lot of their time and take part in serious couponing and plan to print many coupons, it is recommended that one invests in a printer such as a laser printer.

BONUS TWO

SOURCES TO EARN ADDITIONAL INCOME PASSIVELY

Individuals' income can come from a number of sources that are categorized in different categories: active income, portfolio income, and passive income. Passive earning means earning money without working, but that doesn't mean one hasn't worked for it, but they have sewed a seed to have profit in the future.[34] However, some sources tend to be a one-time payment. Just like a long-term investment, one doesn't need to work actively at the time for money. Individuals are looking for ways to earn extra money to fund their retirement plan, reach financial goals, grow savings, replace active income, etc. The main aim of this is not giving up on the day job but to make extra money on the side to make day to day life comfier. An individual earning passive income can boost their work-from-home and be their own boss professional lifestyle.

There are different options available that individuals can adopt as one of the ways to earn passively as a way of increasing their financial income:

Selling products online

---

[34] Pain, George. "Passive Income: Top Passive Income Strategies for the Motivated who want Financial Freedom and Make Money While Sleeping (Volume 1)." (2017).

This is one of the easiest and simplest way of earning additional income passively. Selling products online is a simple business model where an individual can create a sales page or a website to sell the identified products.[35] Today with the increased technology, customers are purchasing a product online without having the need to visit the actual store. The product can either be clothes, an eBook, etc. However, one has to optimize the website and create traffic. The more traffic a website has, the more one can reach out to a wider number of the target customer. There are various options available at online selling, e.g., Digital products, affiliate marketing, drop shipping, automated reselling, etc. Affiliate marketing is the most common in this section. This is where one sells products that have been created by someone else and earn a commission for every purchase. Most of the companies want to sell their products in any way possible, which makes the strategy an effective strategy to earn extra cash.

Dividend stocks

Dividend stocks are another way of earning passively. They are a distribution of a portion of a company's profits. Dividend stocks have been a profitable business for many of the investors in the global market. As organizations generate profits at the end of every financial year, a portion of the earning is funneled back to the investors in the form of dividends.[36] In some cases, one can decide to use the money or either reinvest to increase the stock. However, it is important to note that the yields vary

---

[35] Rambhia, Shruti. "Make Your Own Website to Earn Money Online: 15 Ways To Make Money Online Through Niche Websites! (Create Website Earning Money Online)–Volume 1." (2015).

[36] George (2015).

significantly from one firm to another and can easily fluctuate. This calls for a lot of research to identify the paying dividend stocks that one can choose to ensure that the right one is picked. Moreover, to earn a substantial amount of money, one has to invest in a significant amount of money. Building a high dividend stock portfolio helps create a regular passive income on an annual basis, which can get higher than the money invested in a bank[37]. Dividend-paying stocks, ETFs, and other investments like Fund rise and Lending Club are helping people earn money around the clock. With the possibility of capital appreciation, one can earn a substantial amount of money.

Real estate

Investing in real estate falls in the category of semi-passive income. This is because the investment in this sector is always a little bit of an active venture since there is still work required to be done. A lot of individuals only think of only the rental property, which is out of reach for many. However, this is a sector that requires a lot of research. The information that one gets from the real estate market helps one to pick out the best possible market to hold income as they identify property listing with good cash flow.[38] In real estate, there are different ways that one can earn passively from REIT dividends. Real estate investment trusts are privately or publicly traded firms that pool investors' money to acquire and manage multiple commercial real estate properties, real estate ETF dividends, crowdfunding,

---

[37] Wunder, Haroldene. "The Perils and Pitfalls of Passive Foreign Investment Company Ownership." *The CPA Journal* 89, no. 1 (2019): 48–53.
[38] Haroldene, (2019).

rental property to performing mortgage notes.[39] Therefore, one can identify one of the portfolios to invest in.

Peer to peer lending

P2P lending is a way of lending money to individuals who don't qualify for traditional loans. An individual can earn extra cash from lending to other individuals online and earn something from the interest charged. The platform connects lenders with potential borrowers across the financial market. It enables one to obtain loans directly from another person, cutting out the financial institution such as banks as the middleman. The P2P lending companies often offer their services online and attempt to operate with lower overheads to provide the services more cheaply than traditional financial institutions.[40] As a result, the lender can earn high returns compared to the savings and investment products offered by institutions such as banks. Although the P2P lending is unsecured personal loans, its unique characteristics make its one of the most considered alternative source of financing, especially to the low and middle-income earners. This makes it a good strategy for one to earn extra cash. On the other hand, due to the high number of individuals depending on these online lending platforms, one can obtain high returns relative to different investment types. Moreover, it offers loans with low-interest rates due to the level of competition, thus attracting more customers.

---

[39] George (2017).

[40] Carolan, Michael. "Capitalizing on financing ecologies: The world making properties of peer-to-peer lending through everyday entrepreneurship." *Geoforum* 102 (2019): 17–26.

Conclusively there are various techniques that an individual can adopt to earn extra cash passively. This will increase an individual's income from that which they earn from their workplace. However, one has to undertake a lot of research prior to starting to ensure that it is a good move. It is also important that one select something interesting.

Bibliography

Ahmed, Kazi Afaq, and Zainab Sarwar. "Consumer Willingness to Use Digital Coupons: A Case of Karachi Market in Pakistan." *International Journal of Experiential Learning & Case Studies* 3, no. 1 (2018): 33–42.

Banthia, Dhananjay, and Sujata Mangaraj. "ALiterature Review on Financial Literacy-APathway for Achieving Financial Freedom." *Siddhant-A Journal of Decision Making* 17, no. 1 (2017): 98–102.

Brounen, Dirk, Kees G. Koedijk, and Rachel AJ Pownall. "Household financial planning and savings behavior." *Journal of International Money and Finance* 69 (2016): 95–107.

Carolan, Michael. "Capitalizing on financing ecologies: The world making properties of peer-to-peer lending through everyday entrepreneurship." *Geoforum* 102 (2019): 17–26.

Choudhary, Vidyanand, and Shivendu. "Targeted Couponing in Online Auctions." *Information Systems Research* 28, no. 3 (2017): 490–510.

Fatoullah, Ronald A., Elizabeth Forspan, Jeffrey P. Gorak, and Sidney Kess. "The Critical Importance of a Power of Attorney for Incapacitated Individuals." *The CPA Journal* 87, no. 5 (2017): 10–23.

Gamst-Klaussen, Thor, Piers Steel, and Frode Svartdal. "Procrastination and personal finances: Exploring the roles of planning and financial self-efficacy." *Frontiers in psychology* 10 (2019): 775.

Gunardi, Ardi, Mochammad Ridwan, and Gugum Mukdas Sudarjah. "The use of financial literacy for growing personal finance." *Jurnal keuangan dan Perbankan* 21, no. 3 (2017): 446–458.

Manns Jr, F. Philip. "Powers of Attorney under the Uniform Power of Attorney Act Including Reference to Virginia Law." *ACTEC LJ* 43 (2017): 149–151.

Melin Emilsson, Ulla, and Agneta Ståhl. "Good personal finances or a strong social capital—on different life conditions of importance for an active life when becoming alone in old age." *European Journal of Social Work* 19, no. 5 (2016): 749–763.

Pain, George. "Passive Income: Top Passive Income Strategies for the Motivated who want Financial Freedom and Make Money While Sleeping (Volume 1)." (2017).

Prices, Mirabegron. "Coupons & Savings Tips. GoodRx." (2019): 5–13.

Rambhia, Shruti. "Make Your Own Website to Earn Money Online: 15 Ways To Make Money Online Through Niche Websites!(Create Website Earning Money Online)-Volume 1." (2015).

Ross, Donald Bruce, Catherine Walker O'neal, Amy Laura Arnold, and Jay A. Mancini. "Money matters in marriage: Financial concerns, warmth, and hostility among military couples." *Journal of Family and Economic Issues* 38, no. 4 (2017): 572–581

Shea, Sheila E., and Carol Pressman. "Guardianship: A Civil Rights Perspective." *A Joint Issue: Guardianship and Surrogate Decision-Making* (2018): 51–56.

Sufian, Beth, James Passamano, and Amy Sopchak. "Legal Issues: Guardianship and Supportive Decision Making." In *Health Care Transition*, pp. 293–299. Springer, Cham, 2018.

Valpak's 2019 coupon engagement survey. www.valpak.com/coupons/home

Wunder, Haroldene. "The Perils and Pitfalls of Passive Foreign Investment Company Ownership." *The CPA Journal* 89, no. 1 (2019): 48–53.

Zimbardo, Philip, Nick Clements, and Umbelina Rego Leite. "Time perspective and financial health: to improve financial health, traditional financial literacy skills are not sufficient. understanding your time perspective is critical." In *Time Perspective*, pp. 9–40. Palgrave Macmillan, London, 2017.

THE REALLY INCREDIBLE AMAZING SILLY THING

THE REALLY INCREDIBLE AMAZING SILLY THING

Guy Armstrong

The Nameless Publisher

Published by The Nameless Publisher Tapui Limited AKA Incredibly Condescending Snooty and Pompous Richie-Rich People's Publishing House

"Actually it's just one dude in his mum's basement"

Copyright 2019 by Guy Armstrong AKA Gradually Accostingyoustrong AKA Gratuity Aestheticstrong AKA Grabyabum 'Arrassmentstrong AKA Guycknorris Arseroundhousekickstrong AKA Gi (the ratio of a book's number of sillies per sentence to its cannonballs over the cubic root of its policeman-per-page level) AKA Garnold Arzenneggerstrong AKA Galaxymagic Archmagebong AKA Genius Aristotlestrong

Cover artist:
Times New Roman or some font or whatever

All rights and wrongs reserved

We are fully represented by our legal team Getthemoney Arbitrationstrong.

This book is for my whanau; past, present, future.

ISBN 978-0-473-47533-8

MALCONTENTS

(These can be read in any order, but for maximum fun this book should ideally be read start to finish ...)

HOW NOT TO BE STEPHEN KING

I believe it was the most erudite and very eloquent Thomas Jefferson who once said "There is little of more virtue and worth than days of hard toil, overalls with soil, sweat and work, time spent nagging WINZ to give you enough money for a playstation and heaps of mean-as games, totally bro, get with the times don't be a loser and hook us up with enough cash for some Macca's and K-Fry as well, yeah nah fair dink, drongo."

It is Jeffery Sienfeld's inspirational quote that has inspired me to invest in a new writing crash helmet with visor, some Goretex writing gloves and jacket, a new writing bathtub, some inflatable writing bath toys and hot new lycra writing shorts, a writing playstation and two superdozens of the best writing beer I could find in my neighbour's house. Despite Jefferson D'Arcy's command to get a PS4, use a PS4, become one with a PS4, harden up and get G.T.A. 5 or Bloodborne instead of one of the easy games, I have decided to discipline myself into drinking a few of these writing beers and keyboarding some gnarly blah blah onto the internet, or maybe even just onto some paper like a real old school writer, like Stephen King.

My mates came into my room, and saw me in all my new writing gear.

"You don't have to always be writing" they said, splitting their infinitives without even caring about the craft. "You're not still trying to be the next Stephen King, are you?"

I didn't want to face what they may have meant with such a comment. With shaking hands I took a long, sobering swig of Stephen King brand coffee, and put my mug that was inlaid with a picture of Stephen King's face on the table inlaid with a picture of Stephen King's face. I looked at the Stephen King false passport I had had specially made, and wondered if the pretend deeds to Steven Kyng's house would work according to plan. I checked out my Stephen King skin graft in the mirror and felt the extra plastic vertebrae one of my tradie mates had hammered into my back. "I sort of am Stephen King, a bit" I said, a bit.

But it didn't feel quite right and I wasn't sure if it was an open, honest direction in Lifey McLifeyballs for me. I was sure I would abandon it. The surgeries had been expensive and tiresome, and though I looked like Stephen King, I still didn't have any bestsellers out there bestselling. My books had taken an opposing style, I believe it due to some geographical hemispheric factor, that I in the southern part of earth had not taken into account. Some anomaly no doubt related to the magnetism of our planet meant that my books almost appeared to be competing amongst themselves for position of worstseller, while Stephen King from the northern hemisphere seemed to be enjoying book sales flying home for all seasons. I wondered if perhaps I needed some kind of reverse magnetic advertising-and-money-charger on each of my books in order to counterbalance the poor sales that were obviously caused by the strange geomancies of the southern hemisphere and totally not by an improper or unprofessional ratio of writing beers to writing skill.

"Dude, can you hurry up so we can party?" my mates asked.

I switched gears to proofreading one of my more autobiographical pieces focussed on how much I've matured over the years. Like a superb and resonant champagne, I've improved with time. This essay was a testament to my own emotional growth and the dignified gentleman I've gradually become. I needed to finish it quickly because me and my mates were in a hurry getting to town so we could get really wasted and vandalise everything.

It would no doubt take my mind off a debilitating sadness caused by a horrendous tragedy. My old friend Albert of the Royal New Zealand Army had recently become unemployed and dead at the same time when he was fired from his job as cannon safety supervisor, when he was fired from his cannon.

To help, my friends asked me how my current writing was going. I told them that some of my characters were in a difficult situation because of plot complexities and incoherencies. I thanked them for offering to help me out with story structure. I was almost tempted to take the dark path, and plagiarize, but they held me back. As a principled man, upholding the most honorable whateverish beery blah blah of writing, I must not plagiarize.

"Can I just swipe most of a wicked gun fighting scene or something out of someone else's work, and just change it up a *little*?" I asked them. "You CANNOT do that" my mates said, emphatic in their stance. Still,

I thought it would have been cool to put my creative writing lessons to work and shoot all my characters out of a cannot.

We wanted to party. To save petrol, we took my canoe into town. To save beer, we drank the petrol. We all had issues with various addictions. A problem for many years had been our alcoholism; as well as our propensity to squeeze into tight places, our co-holeism as we called it. We also ranted and raved nonstop about religion and politics, all fifteen of us trying to convince each other of the one real truth, or all fifteen contradicting versions of it. This constant nagging was a strenuous issue for us, this belligerent cajolism.

Naturally I was a little worried about overuce. We all peer pressured and beer pressured each other into the tight space of the canoe, where we were so sweaty and smelly and so close to our kin we said "oooo".

It had been such an ordeal getting my beautiful canoe road legal. The bureaucracy had made almost all of my savings, and my spare time, sail away. They really oar me down. I told them they just about starb'd me to death. I mean the frustration almost keeled me. I sure won't be boating for them next election year, not even Grant Rowboatson. They're really nauty. It took so many years out of my life, I felt I may as well maritime.

My friends weren't much help on the trip to town. While they fought passionately over which great songs to play over the canoe speakers, they would not stop arguing and preaching to me their philosophical and po-litical beliefs about rectifying societal ills via mainstream as well as rather obscure and probably debunked '-isms', and there was a lot of confusion and din, as well as stopping and starting songs and arguments as I had to tell them to stop rocking the boat while they rocked the boat.

By the time we arrived at our favourite bar it was very late and the party had hit a lull. I proudly announced to an excited crowd and entourage, a full bar of dancing people, that because I was so happy to be there, I would buy a drink for everyone at the bar. This was received with great applause and enthusiasm, and the party began again in full swing as I readied my plastic. However, a heated argument erupted and we were thrown out once I began explaining that what I had *actually* meant – which was perfectly clear from what I had said – was that I would buy *ONE* drink which everyone could share, provided there were enough straws to keep things hygienic and people lined up politely. My offer was rejected, and I don't mean to sound paranoid but I did think for a second that the party sounded almost more fun from outside when my entourage left the bar. Perhaps because our debates on making the world a happier, more peaceful place were becoming domineering and almost violent, and were drowning out the funky dance music.

My canoe could not accommodate the beer cans, beer breath and beer-guts of fifteen drunkards, and even though I was very sober, my driving ability was compromised by one night's wear and tear on the suspension. The Kluon ombyoppity was festering a good 3 ml. out of line from the rudder-view mirror, and some crow had built a nest under the brake pedal. It also turned out that my plodge had run out of hee-haw rods.

Police appeared. My mates of course tried to capitalize on this, invoking police power to remove political problems, yet this failed to get off the ground for two reasons. The first being that all of my friends had changed their philosophies this night, deeming another's point of view more logical, more worthy, more convincing and sensible than their own; though as individuals they still contradicted each other and could come to no agreement. This gave the police conflicting information on potential corruptions of leadership. My friends' desire to convert others to their way of thinking had backfired, as each was converted to the belief of the person they were attempting to convert – all my friends, it seemed, were better suited to arguing on the *de*fensive. The second reason was because I sounded drunk when I asked the plod for a spare plodge.

I explained to the police that we were sensible gentlemen even though there had been a slight confusion on the drive through town to the next bar featuring our choice of music. While simultaneously arguing over various speed metal bands and discussing the intricacies of New Zealand's road rules I had for a few intersections confused 240 bass drum beats per minute – b.p.m. – with kilometres per hour – k.p.h., a mistake easily made by a person involved in heated multiple conversations while driving under the influence of politics and thrash metal. I was only driving on the footpath because previously I had been holidaying in Asia and had brought back to New Zealand some of the more ambitious, assertive driving styles reminiscent of Kuala Lumpur and Saigon. Perhaps it could be argued, I argued, that while the police were correct about the speeding and had the radar records to prove it, correct about the driving on the footpath and had eye witness testimony to prove that; was all this attention to detail, evidence-gathering and requirement for psychiatric assessment not simply police correctness gone mad?

The police dragged me out of the canoe, which ruptured my snug fit amongst the bloated beergut air inside with my friends still burping their slurred, bleary opinions, and I felt like I was being dribbled out of a cannon.

My instant fear of the police completely ruined the peaceful post-holiday aftermath I had as a result of also visiting my mate's new-age healing bakery, where he had kneaded my doughy muscles and rolled my mind free through his grinding mental mills, in Arizona where the rock strata tower so high. I was so serene and calm after he literally kibbled me out of his canyon.

But now, that was gone. I didn't like it when the policeman called me bro, I thought it was unprofessional. I actually took him to court for police brotality. They also implied I was fat, which was really hurtful. I told them I had glandular and sugar metabolism problems caused by the last time they beat me up. I told my lawyer they gave me dire beaties.

The judge reprimanded me for my ill health, refusing to believe my claim that it was actually the police's fault: because I'd been arrested so many times, I was suffering from copper poisoning. Because of the damage done to my canoe, I set my lawyer on getting some repair rations. "I'm traumatized because the police violently shot me out of my canoein' your honour" I told the judge.

In court telling my side of the story I could barely keep my composure, or what us death metal musos have, my decomposure. My mates picked me up outside court. The canoe was confiscated and we took a taxi back to my place for shenanigans and recuperation. My mates argued politics and philosophy all the way back; it turned out they had all seen the light of their original positions; and convinced by arguments they themselves had espoused previously they had gone back to being adherents of that which they originally believed. In terms of the evolution of belief, growth had been totally circular.

Somehow it all reminded me of my ex-uncle Jim Allaflamestrong, twice removed, who was twice removed when he forgot to let go throwing away his rubbish and accidentally incinerated himself; then in accord with his will and his fastidious lawyer's insistence, we cremated him.

HOW I RIGHTED A BOOK

An out of place book on my shelf was a little left of the others; I quickly righted it. If I had fancy guests come over, I didn't want them to see how termites had eaten little wormy highways all the way from just about every bit of the bookcase through my extensive horror collection. "I guess all roads *do* lead to *Under the Dome*" I said.

Now if you combine our total sales, me and Stephen King have sold HEAPS of books. *Together*, when we *unite* our overall work spanning *both* our careers, our sales and popularity have blah blahed and yeah yeah yeahed to *so* many people.

Unfortunately for Stephen King and Stephen King's publicist, Stephen King hasn't been the only Stephen King Stephenly Stephen Kinging around in my Stephen King mind.

What's it like being a successful writer like Stephen King? Well... to be totally honest with you... I'm just not sure. Stephen King seems to Thomas Ligotti the Dean Koontz out of people. Whereas a lot of people complain that my books... it hurts my pride to say it... my books... just make them groan.

This has made market penetration quite difficult, even in all of the Stephen Kinglish-speaking countries. I've been writing really hard for so many years, but... it just hasn't happened yet... I've never actually been... with a fully groan publisher.

What was I doing wrong? What was I doing right? Why were all these books in my computer and not in bookstores getting turned into money?

I blame an uncertain amount of my lack of publishment on my old high school English teacher... if I had a better teacher I'm sure I'd be published by now! Why wasn't the vocalist from *Slayer* my English teacher? I would have learnt heaps of cool stuff from him! I bet he never has to put up with people going to sleep in his classes! I went to a *Slayer* lecture once and everyone was wide awake, all mashing into each other and getting into it! The class had actually *memorised* parts of the lecture, and lectured along! In terms of educational organization, it was a totally different learning environment. Some of the teachers were even allowing *beer* in the lecture! The students were so confident in their knowledge of the course that some of them were testing their ability to remember even under all manner of inhalant. Everyone must have learned *heaps* of English there! The microphone was turned up really loud, and the vocalist was yelling every single thing he said, I mean *that's* obviously the right shouty intensity some of our English teachers need to be using to teach the impetuous youth of today.

Books have always been a part of my life, ever since about ten minutes or twenty-five years ago when I wanted to be a writer. Or some time when I clicked on this guy's website, or whatever. The book you're reading now is a milestone of such work and meticulous effort, and hopefully a perfect amount of writing beer.

Before getting too deep into adventures, I must say that my friends and family have spent their time performing as an editing team; they as well as the professional editor I've consulted are owed a debt of gratitude for their efforts. I need to thank them for removing all of the content in this book that was ethically and morally incorrect, overtly perverse, offensive, disgusting, rude, crude and tasteless, or just plain bigoted, backwards and idiotic. After that I need to thank myself for putting it all back in.

Doing writey blah-blah has helped me address my burgeoning mental health issues. I have been recovering from a horrendous tragedy. It will help you empathize when I tell you that in some parts of the writing of this book, I was struck by grief and lost concentration thinking about my dyslexic friend William; tragically he "hospitalized" himself shooting himself into a cannon. From listening to the paramedics I've estimated he *completely* failed his constitution saving throw and did *at least* five critical hits worth of damage to his neck, almost as much damage as I did to mine when I went to that herbal-tincture-preparation themed metal band, *Dripped Baked and Dangled*.

"You mean you *hospitalitied* yourself" I said to William, proudly correcting his broken English. He gave a little shake of his head, the dyslexic's way of saying yes. I was ashamed I had not been there for him in his time of need, none of our circle of friends had. As an experienced headbanger, I felt I could have helped him out with my moshpit experience if I had known he was risking chiropractic reassembly by playing around with sonic assault and ancient artillery. Injuries of the head and neck are preventable, even under intense pressure and loud noises. I can only guess, but I think his problem had been that he had put no mid-air focus on windmill rhythms and beer-drenching prior to neckxertion. Poor William: one of the boys, but ever the loner. *Of course I felt guilty!* If only I had been there for him, I could have kept time with a clique track. Then again, maybe there was nothing any of us could have done. I later heard that he was not using proper safety gear, not even a traditional 1980s sleeveless denim jacket that stunk of old ciggies.

He tried to talk, and coughed a splutter of syllables at me. My ears tried and failed to correct his croaken English. "Doctor, can you save him, *quick*?" I asked the quack, who spake back: "I don't quite have the knack to replace the nick out of his neck, such work is a timely trek."

I was sobered by the doctor's honesty: "There's been *at least* twenty-five hit points of damage, and that's just to his Adam's Apple alone." How precise the arrow of fate had hit! Poorest William - "tell, is there a cure?" I asked while I basked and he tasked. "Maybe better friends would prevent these foul neck-bends."

I got guilting as William's mother sat quilting, her son's vertebrae wilting. I almost couldn't *believe* God or Stephen Hawking or whatever DM had rolled 3d20 for damage with his cannon.

William looked up at us, but he could only see the floor. Good thing I had brought him something to read, a copy of *Neckst Magazine* from the hospital café. I also gave him one of my self-written self-edited self-printed self-published books to read; it hadn't sold well and I have a carton in my wardrobe. "I can't understand a word of this weird garbage" William said, a dyslexic's way of saying he could appreciate every word of some pretty mainstream quality. He tried to give it back to me, a dyslexic's way of saying he really really wanted to keep it. I couldn't figure out why it hadn't done well in the bookstores. William is still with us, though his injury has crippled his future: he is now only able to nod along to slow goregrind, his neck simply cannot accommodate traditional black metal. That is, until we selotaped some really fast buzzing dildos onto his head to help him keep up in the mosh.

After William, I was inspired. I promised myself I wouldn't make the same mistakes other writers often make. A potential problem is that some books have too many characters. For instance, *The Phone Book* has FAR too many. The whole book – and it's HUGE – is spent just introducing all the characters, and they don't even *do* anything! There's no plot! It's so *boring!* And the order that the characters come into the story is really weird and sort of strangely predictable... I couldn't *quite* put my finger on why... it gave me such a familiar feeling, but there was definitely some kind of pattern to it I think. I reckon if they do a sequel I could probably predict the ending. I'd like to give you a proper review, but I don't think it's really worth *anyone's* time. In short: too many characters and not enough plot. Totally convoluted – by the time I read to the end I'd completely forgotten heaps of the characters at the start, and had to back-track just to remember them all! Not a convenient, reader-friendly way to tell a story. I don't know how many hours I spent remembering and learning all the characters in *The Phone Book* but I won't read it again, and I'm certainly not as pumped about the sequel that's coming out next year as the Wellington City Council. About halfway through I read a synopsis online, just to see if it was going to get any good, not that I'm into spoilers or anything. Turns out it's actually a series, so maybe I'm suffering because I didn't read the one before, but in a good series you should sort of be able to pick it up any year, right? Anyway, the plot was a bit too thin for an action guy like me, I need some explosions and gunfire and vindictive passionate backstabby dramas while I'm having a nice quiet, peaceful read.

One of the books I've read was called "Colin's World Atlas" and I thought it was going to be a massive epic, you know? It was big, expensive, and it started out real cool, with all these huge land masses everywhere. They all had cool names like "Africa" and "Canada" and I was like "Yeah, set up the fantasy world, man" – it had a *very* strong start but it was like that *all the way through!*

The faults with *Colin's World Atlas* was this: too far away. In a fantasy novel, it's cool to make up some wacky mythical kingdom and all, but you need some *characters* too. Pictures can often be neat, but these pictures were too far away to SEE anyone, you know? I was getting into the world so much, I got halfway through the novel and realized there wasn't even a main character! Where was all the sword fighting and parties?

What else can we learn from this atlas novel? *You don't have to get TOO geeky about your world.* Is this *Lord of the Rings*? Mate you are not Tolkien, or George Martin, you are just boring old Colin. You haven't even put your last name on the book! I mean come on Colin, you don't even have a blacksmith, you don't even say how many hit dice the monsters in the forests have, you don't even point out which volcanoes the dragons come from. That's unprofessional! But you spent all your time creating this magical world, and there's no *characters* in it! Where's all the dynasties and pirates? Get it TOGETHER, Colin!

Putting stuff like humidity, population size per square inch and stuff like that is a bit too academic for the average reader. Hurry up and get to the action bits already! And the book is too big as well, I mean the editor should have said something. This is one of those extremely rare micro-occasions where you should use an editor.

I totally shrugged off that Randy atlas. It's no wonder that *The Phone Book* and *Colin's World Atlas* were on the same shelf next to each other at the university library. You can see that writing is not only creative, it is hard work, especially with all of that sitting down. After all, *Under the Dome* wasn't written in a day (I think it took him about a day and a half).

HOW TO WRITE A NEW BOOK

A lot of people complained that my new book was too much like my old book, which had been a harrowing account of my life, my marriage, with other people. My new book on the other hand, was *totally* different – *this* one was all about how I was wheelbarrowing a huge amount of my emotional social media baggage onto other sheeple.

I began my new book around the time I was just finishing up some legal hassles I had when I published a whole series of horror books set in Maine under the name Steven King, with a 'V' instead of a 'PH'. All of this became a powerful learning experience I strongly vowed to never ever *ever* again repeat.

I moved on, securing contracts wherein I would supply high schools with more academic aspects of my work. This turned into a second pitfall and powerful money-loser. It was also a powerful learning experience, mainly when it came to remembering to refresh my printer settings as I published thousands upon thousands of extensive chemistry volumes that had to be returned and ultimately destroyed; no school would pay me a cent as these were accidentally *also* printed with 'V's instead of 'pH's.

It reminded me of my old mate Dave whose chest exploded from watching too much wrestling with his older brother, a bully who tried out the moves on poor Dave. Doctors said Dave had simply experienced too many Bret the Hitman Hart attacks. Though when Dave saw a specialist, it became apparent that he suffered from an angina within a pulmonary arrhythmia within his meso-aortic sheath, buried deep behind two other people's further anginas; what the doctors called a myocardial inception.

I must have been stressing about Dave way too much when I secured the contract for some extremely important printing for my local university and Dave the D-man found his way into my work; this on top of the memory problem I had completely forgotten about. I burned all my professional bridges when the post-nominal "Ph.D." was absent from every candidate. Instead, because of my printing error, the names on their graduation certificates were followed by the letters "V.D."

Career-wise, I was decimated. My name was not only mud, it was cowpat, algal bloom and bird-crap-on-a-flash-car. After that mistake my future felt of biblical-level genocide like when the Israelites got really into their bows and arrows and shot everyone out of the land of Canaan.

To deal with the absolute brutality of emotion I was feeling, I decided to spend a bit more time drowning my sorrows with my new flatmate, Brent. The police pulled me over when they saw I had bought one of those crazy machines that was used in the massive gnarly parties that eventually ended in the epic beerheading of the French monarchy, a suillotine.

"Blleeuurk!" I vomited. "Step out of the vehicle, please Slur" said the slurgeant. They inquired about all manner of splotches throughout my vehicle. I thought they were being quite derogatory and unfair in some of their implications. I told them that as I was a gentleman who understood the importance of attention to detail, prior to my time as a student I had been a prestigious and well-respected splotch-maker. My mates doing keg-stands in the back of my vehicle were *not* an unpaid labour force, they were splotch-making purely for joy and nostalgia. The skeptical police threw me on the ground and slammed my wrists into the cuffs, ripping one of my best blleeuurk shirts. "Oh your handcuffs do squeeze" I told the poleeze. I didn't have time to go to jail, I explained, as it was getting to about that time of year when us writers go into a deep hyphen-ation. "Sir, please stop being so pernicious" said the pernice. I didn't want to spend an entire hyphen-ation season in jail again, and I hoped my lawyer had brought in all the usually wet replies that had been hanging outside on the proseline.

It was largely my own fault that there were so many police in my life. Though I was a conservative gentleman, because of my somewhat excitable nature and frequent road usage, I found it hard to give them any real reason for movement out of my life's otherwise banal tract. As much as I respected the police and the work they performed in keeping us safe, I was very constablepated.

A highlight of this was being pulled over one afternoon by a rather amazing policewoman; intelligent, conversant and attractive in all those personal ways that make someone special and unique. While I discussed my thoughts on whether there was any meaning to life she nodded and listened intently, something I would never have expected from a bill-ociffer. I showed her my really cute kitten with nits I took driving; surely a purr-lice-woman would like that. Attracted as I was, I began bragging to her about my record collection, and my arrest record collection. She was unimpressed, and went ballistic. It hurt deeply, as any hope of time spent together – a date, a lunch, a getting-to-know-each-other – was submerged in a *terrifying* trauma when she drew her service revolver and threatened to shoot me right out of my Toyota Cannonmry. She slammed my face into the dirty road-gravel, demanding I accompany her to the Police Department where she would school me like a little kid.

"I'm not interested in some kind of P.D.'a'trician, Ma'am" I said. She arrested me for being too empathetic. "Empathetic" is when a writer doesn't used the letter "M" enough in their work, which the poncy literary types think is just pathetic. My lawyer was preparing a defence in which he would argue that because of my upbringing I was unfamiliar with the posher sections of the alphabet, but had been attending yeah-nah-versity for a few years to sort of chill out and maybe look at them a bit when I wasn't at the pub.

It helped ease any tension I had when I got to know some of the cops down at the station on a first name basis. They actually seemed pretty cool, even going so far as to introduce themselves while they got ready to throw me in front of the judge: "Hi, I'm Constable Pat, this is Ted." Although I was suddenly less popular when I told one of them that the police were arresting me so often they were at risk of being a dick, Ted.

In an effort to convey my own point of view, I told the judge of the harrowing, anguished accounts of my working life on the street, wherein a tradesman of ill repute and no morals had been trying to get us impressionable young men hooked on the crack that he was peddling around some of the building sites in our poor neighbourhood. I spoke of the incredible, *nauseating* adrenalin rush I had when he was almost looking at me wrong with his brown eye. Partly for my own protection, but also for pure street vengeance I had popped a backwards cap on his ass the next time he bent over. The jury was mortified to hear it was a Brumbies cap, and that I already knew he was a Penrith fan. This, on top of the Canadian bro who came over threatening everything of not much value in our messy rooms, by telling us young men to hurry up and get our mums to tidy our rooms. My lower lip wobbled as I told the jury what had to be done to survive in my part of the world.

The judge offered me a get-out-of-jail-free card if I stopped being a public nuisance and did my best to end any tension I had with law enforcement, and so I reluctantly agreed to drop my eighty-million-dollar defamation suit against the policeman who had inappropriately referred to me as "dude" when I didn't even have my surfboard with me.

Some on the force didn't buy my apology. They thought I was still just a selfish, negative gentleman blotting out life's joy like a mountainous wart. They basically thought I was a nah-Sir-cyst. I think they were concerned I had that terminal illness, can't-Sir, because that's what I kept on saying as they told me to drive in a straight line on the road like everyone else.

In court it was going well until I accidentally opened my big mouth and referred to the judge as *dude-yo-wotup-uce-yo-yo-yo-'sup-ma'a'fa'a'-my-*

Limpest-Bizkit-my-Wu-Tang-clansman. I awaited with incredible trepidation the harsh sentence and punishment. The judge said my antics were the result of a sort of social immaturity and were really quite unimpressive. I did not tell him about my great aunt Helen whose claims of levitation were so unimpressive they didn't even need to be seen to be disbelieved.

It really hurt my feelings and threw me off a lot when the judge patronized me. He explained to the court that no-one should be offended by me, that I was just a bit backwards. I wanted to challenge this, and was tempted to tell him about my great grandfather Osric, a man who had lived his entire life backwards. He outdid any luddite in his backwardness, eschewing progress and living in reverse with such determination and intent that while he was born in the year 1904 he actually died in 1821.

The judge told the court not to worry about me, he said I was just a nobody. I did not tell him about my great uncle Alfonse, who became such a nobody that instead of dying, one day in the old folks' home he had simply decided that he would cease to exist. As a child hearing this I was sad, yet also elated – freed of one incredible fear when I realized that his church could no longer have him cannonized.

HOW TO WRITE A NEW ARTICLE

A lot of people complained that my new article was too much like my old article, which had been all about my sparrowing dive into a great mound of law enforcement, literally a police-hill. My new article, on the other gland, was about my Grandfather's narrowing squirts of incontinence without a pee pill.

"Sir, please step out of the pelican" said the pelicman. I hoped he was unaware I had not paid the government's ostentatious new petrel tax. I asked if I was illegally parked or driving, or whatever, along this avianue. "Stop pulling me over, *sheeesh*!" I told the poleeesh. It reminded me of the opposite of the time when I was taking my submarine for a hoon and the police pulled me under.

I explained to police that *actually*, what I was **actually** doing was driving in **actual** accordance with fully legal actualities provided one superimposed a "non"-actual yet tenuous international political-religio-scientific-emotional mapping upon an 'actual' two-dimensional – actual

– roadway; and that actually this was a much superior way to actualize the vehicular tradition.

The police hauled me off to court, charging me with probably being one of those people who would enroll in PHIL 101 because he thought he would enjoy it instead of just enrolling in it for the points, like a normal student. The police also told me I was one of several people in the community that they had suspected for quite some time was using the word "actually" far too much in conversation, and charged me with actualling a police officer.

After we did the paperwork I sat on the station steps, a little sad and listening to my ghetto blaster in a stoopendous, horrendous, life's agony. I was lucky that my situation was better than some. My friend and now flatmate Brent was also feeling metaphorically run over by the huge-end ass of life's wagonny. His issues were multiple and complex. Both of his legs had horrendous deformities. One leg was longer than the other, and the other leg was shorter than the other.

Years earlier his extended family were celebrating the release of his father from a retreat for people with chronic depression; upon his release he looked forward to life with optimism, seeking work in a circus – a safe and happy place one would think, for recuperation. Brent was just a baby, no doubt he would enjoy visits to his father's work growing up – this at least was their hope for the future. Much of their large family had attended to see the crowning achievement of his new life, his proverbial rise from the ashes. Yet a sudden bout of depression struck, and while he was waiting to be shot out of the cannon, he shot himself.

The loss of Brent's father was not the only hardout ship he and his mother faced. His birth was one of the fastest in history, with hundreds of midwives and doctors writing articles in prestigious medical journals about him literally exploding from his Irish mother, Mrs. O'Gannon.

One of Brent's childhood traumas had to do with emulating the lion tamers he would have seen at the circus. He had been joy-riding his dog in the park one day, and putting his head in his pet's mouth in between racing and games... until some other dogs came along, and with all their distractions and butt-sniffy barking, Brent was shot completely out of his canine.

He gradually became a solitary man, and kept to himself. I still cared though. Getting in touch with his stepfather, my only connection to my friend, was a difficult and horrendous agony. Brent's stepfather worked at the Ministry of Conversation, in the Department of Accidentally Transferring People's Calls to the Wrong Department. He was eventually transferred to the Department for Keeping People on Hold as Long as Possible, however this was an *unintended* 'unintended' mistake, not the work of the recently restructured Department of 'Unintended' Mistakes, as he had actually been more trained toward resignation in the Departing Department.

To me, Brent's entire life looked like a portendous chagrinny. Brent had very poor eye-brain-foot coordination and was terrible at getting to where he needed to be. His sense of direction was constantly that of someone on multiple yaw benders, all flagonny. Thus I admired him deeply for persevering in his work as a geography lecturer. We also had similar music tastes, with Brent being a lifelong fan of that cartography-compost-applecore band *Behind Orchard Spill*.

Before living with me, Brent had lived in the wrong house. He paid for a larger, more spacious and comfortable property while he squatted in a neglected hovel. This happened because he confused the house numbers on the street – the big house he was paying for at one end, number ninety-one; and the grotesque derelict thing in which he mistakenly squatted at the other, number nineteen. He complained about his high rent for poor quality, yet anguished over the empty-looking large town-house in which he was entitled to live every time he drove past it and back past it again in the other direction, every day on the wrong way to work. I suppose we were both a bit bird-brained sometimes. But no wonder I worried about Brent and his wacky problems of sanity, his tendency to say cluck and be gannetty.

Brent didn't like his squatting-mates either, they incessantly argued, face-to-his-face and via a cohort of notes on the refrigerator. The place was infested and rotting, and they all haggled over nonsense while suffering endless mosquitoes. Brent was so happy when I offered him a room at my place away from all the horrible squalor tics.

When he first came to me, he appeared so emotionally frozen, so cold inside, that I wondered if he was still my brrrrrro. He was in a slump. I told him about my other flatmate who was slowly learning to bake but not very good at it, and had pulled his loaf from the oven too early. While it tasted fine it hadn't risen, and sat on the table looking rather saggy. I told Brent to help himself in case he wanted slumpthing to eat.

He doubted himself and asked me if he could perceive accurately, did I think him clever? I assured him seriously that he, like myself I hoped, was for sure a very intelligent Brentleman. We were close even though he was a little eccentric, and I was proud to be a part of his inner quirkle. Though sometimes he pissed me off, and we almost came near bromestic violence. Of course my hair receded while living with him; I began suffering from pullme'airy hyperBrentsion.

I punched Brent in the guts really hard one day, and he screamed and cried that half his stomach, including the little bit at the end, had come out. Brent wanted revenge. He thought he would get up and be a dick to everyone, including me. But I did not like Brent's up-and-dick-to-me. I was furious with Brent when I found he had sublet my basement to a dirty little man named Tim, who made all manner of naughty videos down there. I implored them I could not stomach it. They forgave me, trying to appease my anger. But I did not like Brent's up-in-dick Timmy.

A powerful factor in Brent's life had been the bullying he had always experienced from his largely male peers. Horrendously tragically it had been stupendously magically it had been constant from childhood to adulthood in every neighbourhood and it wasn't good. Though I felt I had feedback enough to help him, I couldn't quite put a delicate explanation together, so I said nothing as he told me that he couldn't fathom why people made such fun of him; while he put on his winkle pickers and his knickerbockers and got ready to take his mum to the Michael Bolton gig.

I had other issues besides Brent and his mental health problems. I'd had wonky teeth since childhood, and a spat of burping noises had kept me from the dating scene of late. I went to an orthodontist to have my teeth and mouth fixed, but accidentally went to an unorthodoxdontist, who simply added to my dental and belch problems.

We were two friends who like kick-boxers, knee did each other. Thank goodness Brent moved into my flat, my small bedsit on the outskirts of right in the middle of town, away from all the hustle and bustle of the constant, stressful suburban pursuit of relaxation.

A few weeks after he moved in, there were disgusting wet noises from the carpet all through the house. Brent seemed unable to take a straight route home and ended up in muddy forest walks all the time, even though he took his car. He trampled all manner of sloppy dirt through my home.

I had hoped Brent could help me address some teething problems I was having with my writing, but he completely failed as an authordontist. He felt worse for it, and his depression spiraled even deeper into the depths of despair. He was already saddened by his rental and wealth problems. He cried and cried, making the carpet even wetter, dislodging the floorboards and glue under the linoleum as he stomped in tantrum, which only added to my Brental and squelch problems.

5

HOW TO BE CAREFUL ON THE INTERNET

You bet there is some weird creepy stuff in cyberspace these days. You had best be careful because some of it is quite deviant, borderline sickening, just *freakish* and *not normal*. I know because I made it and sent it to you.

There *are* a lot of really crazy people in the world, right? This is exactly what I said to the police when they pulled over next to me while I was walking along the Desert Road at about 2 a.m. "Sir, step out of the shoes and put your feet where I can see 'em" said the podiatrylice.

I had over time become hungry, eventually famished as I walked the endless twists and turns of empty road in the dead of night, alleviating my anguish by eating the dry vitamins contained in some watercress I passed by, dropping out of a river-borne tree on someone's farm. The police picked me up soon afterwards, no doubt for cresspassing on dry-vit dropperty.

Funny thing is, the police actually told me they were *looking* for a crazy person! I told them I hadn't seen any crazy people in a long time, but they were not on their way again, though I felt my argument convincing. After some verbal grappling, I came clean. It was good they had told me they were looking for a crazy person, as I had just come from a building that was *packed* with crazy people. Some of them were *very* strange. Finally someone had left a door open and I was able to leave! I told the police I had been trying to get out of there for a long time. It hadn't occurred to me that I probably could have *called* the police to help me get out of there! For surely it was not legal to detain someone, straight into a weirdly uncomfortable jacket, against their will? And then force them to eat heaps of pills to make them sane when they weren't even crazy, and to discuss their deepest feelings all day?

"What you'll be doing there is getting back into some medication, you'll be taking a lot of pills" said the pilllice. I wasn't sure about this, I didn't think it was fair.

"Don't you think the people in my life, my friends and family should be involved in these big decisions regarding my thinking and lifestyle?" I asked. "Could I not at minimum consult them and take a poll?" I inquired of the polllice.

"We don't have any patience so get in the car and stay there long enough to get piles" said the pilelice. I told them I had no patience for the impatient, they said it didn't matter because I was an inpatient. I told them I was definitely *not*, with the qualification that if I was any sort of patient it was an outpatient. I argued this with such vehemence I almost became a shoutpatient. "You'll be much warmer in the car with leather seats and heating Sir, not to mention the gentle airflow" said the po-suede-lice. But I did not want to be in-a-car-Sir aerated. "Just get in already" said the persuade-lice. "I don't think I'm either hallucinating *or* crazy or even a bit wacky and eccentric" I told the totally far out cosmic popsychedelice.

I think I managed to confuse them enough because they did eventually take me back to Wellington where I was viciously awfully horrendously agonizingly maliciously sadistically wrongly imprisoned sitting near a desk while they did some paperwork for almost two-and-a-half minutes. I also had to listen to this preachy policewoman tell me that heaps of us young men were ruining the values of the country and were basically dicks. I assured her that the business I had started, EvilGreedyPollution-Corp. Ltd., was in *no way* an immoral or unethical corporation, all about money and power and making environmental stuff worse like everyone else. The police told me to stop blah-blah-blahing but it was so difficult to keep my trap shut. My mother always called me her little blahling. I imagined how cool it would be to escape. "Don't even think about it" said the thought police.

Sometimes the world is in term oil. I remember telling the police about the leadership I was listening to, like Simon Skynet, who has said that children should avoid the internet entirely because they cannot deal with the doper memes.

It all reminded me of the piperidolating anguish I felt at the near loss of my friend Jake, who exploded sky-high from a tall, thin vat of a strange technological substance named crapinon. This happened after he and I went running through a chemical manufacturing plant, banging everything in sight with many hammers in what began as a harmless game of whack-a-mol[-1].

HOW TO GET ARRESTED ON YOUR BIRTHDAY AND THE REALLY POLITICALLY CORRECT THING AND THE DEFINITELY INDECISIVE THING

For my birthday this year, one of my friends got me a copy of *The God Delusion* and another one of my friends got me a copy of *The Science Delusion*. Fortunately I owned neither of these interesting books; unfortunately both of my friends were so excited that I imbibe of their wisdom, and with both of them being quite competitive each had decided they would "get in first" so to speak, which led to them both reading their gifts to me at the same time, while I was driving.

Confusing the GPS directions I had with the layout and sheer intensity of the international scientific and religious spectrum of thought and research, as well as the relevance over arguments regarding the political need for minority groups to be represented, I managed a mostly empty-throttle meander all over the six lanes of Wellington's highway, sometimes barely avoiding being the cause of the automotive equivalent of an extreme immigration occurring between two high-velocity countries.

Disillusioned with all of the Gods I thought were real, and the Sciences I thought were objective, I had found solace in using this birthday opportunity to get swilling some hearty grog with my old mate Swilliam, whose father had no doubt named him such for this exact purpose. His father had been a lifelong fan of that Indonesian trans-Atlantic vomitcore band *Bintang Yorkshire Swill*.

Police on horses approached. "Am I in trouble again?" I asked. "Of course" said the four ofcoursemen. They begged: "could this erring behaviour come to an end, Sir?" But I did not like Sir-end-erring. They demanded to know if I was drinking any funny beverages while I was out driving. I showed them I had only been using dandelion tea-hee-hee. Their wristlock made my hand ill, then they gagged me so I couldn't keep spouting off. I couldn't believe it when they tipped me over and poured me out. "We're still going to have to charge you, Sir" they said. My sneaky lawyer added his surcharge to the Sircharge. *And* I deduced that some tea got in my ear! I hoped they weren't laughing at my intheoryauraltea complex. It was the worst day that year since my histology lecturer tried to pick a fight with me for looking down a microscope wrong.

We kept on drinking as the police put the cuffs on us, a real test of our swillpower. Swilliam was way over the limit at about nine hundred swillometres an hour. Me and my mates weren't out to harm anyone, we were just casual blokes, though hoping one day to party as hard as guys we thought were superbeeroes like Dan Swillbeerian.

It all reminded me of the time I got in touch with my feminine side and went buttercup hunting, only to realize come darkness that I had fallen asleep in the wrong hut. The farmer who owned it not only called me a cissy, but pulled out his rifle and shot me completely out of the long hallway of his cabin.

I couldn't believe it when the policeman called me mate, it sounded so unprofessional I had him dragged in front of the magistmate. Tragically, horrendously, offendously, this policeman also got *completely* away with calling me *oi hey you* before my case was brought again before his magisty.

I apologized for my inconvenient character traits to the magistrait, and for my bad driving, and for the influence of my friends. I apologized, I was so sorry I said, that I had jeopardized the drives of other people. I said sorry for reading two books with two conflicting ideological presuppositions read aloud by two conflicting friends I secretly thought were biasing the emphasis and tone of readings while I was driving in two conflicting directions extremely slowly in six lanes while driving. I said sorry for not being as privileged as all of the fancy judgey prosecutey clever people with too many degrees and law school addictions. I said sorry for going out of my lane and for crashing my vehicle. Of course I said sorry for being born and for existing, and for all the atom-confetti that currently made me having been shot out of God's or non-God's or whoever's or no-one's massive universey spaghettiey big cannon-bang. *"I'M SORRY OK?!"* I shouted. I told them all I would withdraw the atoms with which I would make myself from a completely different Big Bank in my next incarnation.

The police arrested me again, this time for being one of those horrible people who apologize too much. I apologized for being one of the people who apologize too much, then I began apologizing for being one of those *even worse* people who *don't actually mean it* when they apologize and continue doing the thing they were apologizing for, while they apologize for doing it.

The bailiff pulled me over on the edge of the courtroom. "Sir, step out of the apology-mindset please." I was arrested again, for attempted guilt-trip with amateur reverse psychology using non-specific femto-philosophical adjuncts and trying to inflict Kant boorish trauma.

I wasn't even allowed to snack in court. "Put all those snacks away" the boule loaf hors d'ouvred. I explained that when we nearly had the crash, I had really desired to lift up Johnny, a fellow student who was totally my bae, through the sunroof out of harm's way, but my knees on the steering column had been blocked by the rummagey old potato sack I use to do the pedals and I couldn't leverage my full length in the seat to really put my weight behind lifting Johnny, unless I had put my drinks down. As a result, Johnny had received Bachelor's degree burns and the mean Hendrix and Bowie mix on his iPod had been reshuffled out of order. "I still think you should have elevated Johnny up out of harm's way" said the bae lift.

On my way out, he asked me how I would spend my time. I said as a greenie hippy student, proactive in the community, I was going to organize grassroots political activism against the technological influence and corporate dominance over our food supply. "Well I actually do social media public relations outreach for the pesticide industry so I'll be undermining as much of that as I can, thanks for letting me know" said the Bayer Lifter.

"Oh well, I may as well just give up then" I said. "It's cool if I drink in here, right? Huck us a beer, bro!" I shouted to the beer lift. He didn't like me at first glance, and we scuffled. He threw me to the ground and my beer caught on his thighs, ripping his pants and exposing his buttocks. "This is a bit awkward" I said to the bare left.

We stood, sizing each other up. He was right about Johnny, I could have taken better care of my kinny-kin-kin. The bailiff was a giant of a man, royal-purple-skinned and glorious, with rugged stubble all over his chinny-chin-chin. Before he shot me, I told him he was definitely my favourite little biggy.

I told the police it was horrendous agony when I was beaten by a horse, who actually *cheated* at chess. The horse kept on getting the moves wrong, it couldn't move the pieces quite right. "Did you just refer to a horse as 'it'?" belaboured the politically correct people. "Did you just refer to a horse as being wrong?" demanded the groups for Animal Rights. When I jokingly told the extremely serious judge that being beaten at chess by a gardener was a rhododendrous agony he locked me up in solitary.

I think the thing that got me into this mess was that I had said to one of the policemen that upon seeing his horse, I had realised I was actually so hungry that I felt as though I could have eaten maybe not *that* horse, but a silly pantomime horse, maybe not filled with people horsing around but filled with some kind of mushy foodstuff. I wondered if I should have taken my own horse into town, as well as enough food to eat in the shape of a giant horse. By this point I was so tired I could have slept on my mate's horse's couch while it smashed out some Tony Hawk Pro Skater with its opposable hooves that I promised I didn't want made into opposable yummy lollies.

I was so thirsty I could have liquefied and waited for ages, fermented and drunk a less-than-one-hundred-percent pantomime horse. Animal Rights Activists attacked me because I had thought about attacking an animal. Extremely Politically Correct People attacked me because I had referred to an animal as an animal. I ran sprinting, exhausted until my lungs were volcanic. To my dismay, a group of people who were offended by stereotypes started attacking me because I had generalized people's behaviour.

I was still thirsty. I wondered if I could siphon a gallon or two of water out of a camel's hump on the sly without controversy and aggro, without these incredible world-shaping armchair uprisings. I wondered how many needles would be required to poke a hole in a camel and drink its hump, but this was not an acceptable thing in a camel's world-view or dogma, and it kicked me; along with my beliefs on treaty-free hump-colonizing for hydro-extraction I was promptly shot out of its religious canon.

Tragically, the camel had privatized its hump-water. Corporate econo-hydrologists had their extraction needles at the ready. I needn't worry about my own opinions because they and the media were thoroughly giving the situation a gander, real proper. I figured me and my needles had as much chance of getting a drink as a bunch of preachy people arguing over their lifestyle virtues had of turning the world into a heaven.

They said I was different, too old for this new world disorder, too young to fit in with tradition. They said I was shallow, a man with values made of plastic. It was only too fitting that they pushed me into the ocean, where I became vampirically lodged around the neck of a seahorse.

I have no idea how or why I survived. It all reminded me of my mate Nige the physics graduate who told me about the really amazing time he had so much beer that he drank himself to death but the momentum of the beer was so strong that he kept on drinking so that he drank himself back to life, only to horrendously tragically in agony realise his boss was on the phone saying he had to start work early.

MONEY BLAH

You know, I've found it really difficult making the twenty-five dollars I dreamed of owning before I turn a million. I guess dreams are expensive. It is nice when they come to fruition though. After the first half of a difficult year, I have really made progress. I recently finished a three-month ordeal at the engineering faculty, looking into some great structural and aesthetic design work.

And yesterday? I finally duct taped a half dozen set of massive concrete tits onto George, our pet bull. "Those will be pretty useful" I thought.

My GF was also a cantankerous old bovine. She said I had more money than brains. I wondered if such a comparison was possible given the differing nature of money and brain matter, yet for some unknown reason I felt a little anxious and worried as I jingled the forty cents in my pocket.

Still, it was a major achievement for me. I was happy to be out and about again, after having been locked up in the hospital for three weeks with an itchy willy – and you know what that means: surgery, radiation, motorized sandpaper and catheter-whisk therapy, willy-grinders, forty thousand willivolts conduction resistometer jumper leads grip-taped to each willy actuator, some itch-vaccines, maybe a few thousand rpm here and there on the willy-lathe, all the usual stuff. They even stuck one of those tiny cameras up my willyocoecal valve.

Once out, I began looking for work. I'm sure if you've ever been job hunting you'll empathize with me when I say it's been difficult just getting an interview, even though I've put *heaps* of Chuck Norris pictures in my CV.

There were potential dark stormy nights on the horizon for our family, and it was vital that I find employment. My father, an engineer, didn't like the way the auto industry's use of quality electronics was putting him out of work. "They don't break down like they used to" he grumbled.

My situation reminded me of my mate Alf, who was the laziest man in all of New Zealand. So lazy was he that we all believed he was in serious danger of rupturing the procrastinatory matrix that holds the country together, the yeah-nah continuum. In his presence me and the boiz were humbled silent, in awe of how hard he refused to work. Another friend was my mate Joel, Oh, dear dear Joel... who had only lit the cannon's fuse to have something with which he could light his badly rolled cigarette... good ole Joel who had only put his feet in the cannon to keep them warm with the fire, just for a few seconds... poor Joel who had only fallen asleep accidentally because he was suddenly out of the Wellington wind, warm and snug...

How I missed him when I heard he missed the bullseye; a soft landing spot in the farms just out of Cannon's Creek, Porirua. He actually landed on a rock-hard concrete statue of a soft landing spot. It was not the only horrendous tragedy from which someone else had not quite recovered, from which I had not quite recovered. In a magic trick that went horribly wrong, my old mate Barry, a man so undeserving, so soft and sweet, accidentally shot himself out of an aluminium can.

Because I was so broke, my girlfriend suggested I go on welfare. I refused at first, and we suffered for it. Still, we had our dignity as I scrounged for work. I bragged thoroughly about this on social media. My girlfriend was into self-care and good health, and asked me to take her to the *Wellness Fair*. This I did, which caused a little social media confusion when friends saw the event. I was labelled a hypocrite, which hurt my pride. I fought the insults valiantly as I rung food from rags. That is, until my lady enrolled me in *real* welfare. In a bad dream I attended a protest on wealth inequality. "MORE PAY FOR C.E.O.S AND INVESTORS!" I screamed. The activists all glared at me, and I was beaten with placards and equality signs. I began explaining to the activists that no doubt it would trickle down…

What had I become? I woke up in a cold sweat at the welfare office, my lady tugging on my shirt that this was the only way. I didn't want to need the money, but I did want to survive. I was supposed to work anywhere they told me.

I didn't like the first job they sent me to, and tried to avoid it. I wasn't lazy, I said, I repeated, I told them again and again; I was just having some mental health issues that would make working in a cannon factory a little difficult. They didn't like my excuses, which were not based so much on empirical or peer-reviewed research but on my own gut feelings and instinct. My girlfriend was also unimpressed, and this belabored our relationship further. I was dragging her down, dragging both of us down with my fears. I couldn't work, I could barely set foot on the factory floor because of some deep prejudice emanating from within an unknown part of my psyche. I quaked and shuddered every time I came close to the place. I was useless, and then I was fired, and then I was still broke, so I just huddled up into a ball. Because of her short fuse, it wasn't long until my girlfriend shot me out of our relationship.

HOW TO GO AWAY FROM WAR

When I first met her, it was mild attraction at about fifth or sixth sight. My girlfriend had a profile pic where some of her hair drooped down over one of her eyes, and she looked a bit like the drummer from that gore band *Boiled in Rotting Offal*. I think that was what really did it, what prompted me to make the first move... to put my arm round her and ask so romantically if she wanted a bite of my steak 'n' bacon pie. We were indeed a match made in a 7-eleven. In the beginning we went through the usual ceremonial romance depravities. For a time, we were happy together. Until we got too close.

The reign of epic brutal slaying maniacal steamrollering-my-heart war-Satan terror she inflicted upon me began as what appeared to all onlookers as a strong, out of control mood swing, yet somehow felt more like a tactic of deep masterminding, even more difficult to outsmart than Jon Irenicus. Even feistier than the last boss at the end of *Conan* on PS3 set to hard difficulty.

It was totally her-end-us. We were to see no more of each other during the day, *and* the night. I was to sleep on the sofa I had slept on before we were together, yet the way she made this command suggested there was some kind of retribution if I chose to obey it... however I felt a hidden hook in that she instigated that it was *my desire* to return to sleeping there. I assured her it was not, yet somehow I had become the terrorist in her negotiation-free policy.

My fear and emotional over-reaction to the situation may have been due to childhood trauma. I was the victim of an undermining anguish of my own doing. When I was a novice writer still learning the trade, I experienced the incredible pain of a paper cut when my finger was shot out of a Canon printer. I have never fully recovered, and my girlfriend reminded me of it over and over. I hated the way some women just used me because they liked playing with my huge memories.

She was annoyed because I had almost no money, no job that paid enough to survive with dignity. I refused to rid our house of the piles of extraneous junk and mess, feeling this hoard was all I owned beyond the small clippings of nebulous post-decimal digits in my blank account. I did not contribute enough to things around the house. Instead, she claimed, I spent too much time with my alpha male friends. I can't blame her for it, but she empathized so little with the tendency of men to become ensnared in the egotism and bravado of other men. Too often was I simply doing my daily muck-around when I would hear their bragging, the clinking of bottles, the sports and video game statistics, the glugging of wheaty drinks and join in. I knew deep down that all too often I had become caught in the bragnetic field.

I was paranoid my girlfriend was becoming abusive. I think she secretly wanted some kind of role reversal that she outwardly prided herself on claiming to not need. I wondered if the things she said were true, or were they some form of insult ingeniously designed to fly below my intellectual radar?

Nothing was funny anymore. I felt like I couldn't think of any jokes after so many of those "harmless on the outside" statements and reminders that released their barbs upon deeper inspection. Whatever creative eggs I needed for articulate joke gestation were somehow inaccessible. She had basically given me a complete hystericalectomy.

We argued. Over things, over words and their meanings, over possessions we had been given as a couple – the dishes, the jug, the breadmaker, the little statue of the waving microscopist, the mundane appliances. As our relationship retreated from sublime generosity into aggressive independence and separate seflishness, we began taking what we thought was ours from the unity.

"IT'S *MY* BLENDER!" She shrieked at me one day, waving the darn thing above her head, tendons popping out of her elbow. "STOP WRITING DEATH METAL SONGS ABOUT AUGMENTING KILLER ROBOTS WITH *MY* BLENDER! THIS BLENDER IS A *PART* OF ME!" She hated how enthused I was about the object, the way in which even unpopular kitchen implements had become inspiring musically to me, how early and mid-nineties death metal music somehow wormed its way into nearly every conversation – even those about our relationship, while she felt ignored. Why she cared for, and felt such a kinship with a simple blender was beyond me, but such is the power of some gifts that make rad whizzing noises. I walked around the house vowing to cease my constant thinking over my favourite music genre so gingerly in my guilt, like Mel Gibson in the movie *Payback* with his hammer smashed toes.

The carcass of our relationship neared its swansong. She didn't like the way I was polarized – a manly man, yet victimized by simple comments and child's play, while I worried that her tomorrow belonged to a different body than me. She was a stirrer all right. She had stirred tremendous feelings within me at the beginning of our relationship, then dashed them upon the concrete-with-abusive-punk-graffiti-spraypainted-on-it of our souls. The bones of my toes were stirring with rage because of the egg shells I continued to walk upon. She screamed at me that if I didn't tow the line, I would be ousted from the housestead. The passive tense of course, I thought in suspicion, keeping her out of blame's way. I voiced it too. Our honest love together had turned into an Orwellian boot grinding my face – probably both our faces – into mushy peas and gravel. I think there was a time where we both wanted to fix things, and we went on wanting to fix things, even after things were unfixable. But after all that drama I couldn't be bothered with her weird blender dysphoria. I didn't care for her toe stir either.

Did there exist, I wondered, any vital remains of our love? Could we start again? I prayed for some surgical steel, and the youthful gleam of 1985. Then again, perhaps my relationship problems were of a more cosmic origin. I had no idea that the flea was an astrological sign, but sometimes you just have to admit you don't know everything. My girlfriend used our differing star signs as an excuse to excuse herself. She said we were basically incompatible because I was a complete lunar tic.

I couldn't believe our relationship had descended into such abominable putridity. A few weeks prior to the beginning of the end, we had a large party. I believed that since that time my girlfriend had suffered due to the incredible amount of drugs some "friends of friends"-level weirdos had mixed into our herb collection. When she came at me with her accusations, it only made things worse when I said that for a long time, she had been completely dill-luded.

She didn't like my long hair, and she likened me to animals, including stupid ones. She said I was an annoying maney-yak. It all came to a head when I said that her passive-aggressive lies and meanness had become predictable and an ever-repeating pattern like the fibber-nasty sequence I had read about on my mate's new-age website.

She was always complaining about how I loved heavy metal music more than her. How I knew details of musicians, instruments and bands but talked little of the things she and I had in common, not even the idyllic farm we had envisioned for our future in the early days. I couldn't believe she could set fire so callously to the crisp barns of our love and completely change the intensity of our band, so to speak. Then again, maybe it was for the better.

We were so passive-aggressive towards each other. Whatever one of us did, the other insulted by doing the exact opposite. One day she bought a can opener. I couldn't help myself, and the following day I bought a can closer. I didn't tell her that I was secretly still jamming with that kitchen utensil themed military death metal band *Canopenerable Corps*. When she spent hours searching in the forest to find a stray cat, I spent hours searching a bit of old carpet to find a spare tac. She spent hours playing with her new cat, I spent hours with my new tac. She took her cat to the expensive vet to declawed, I took my tac to the expensive engineer to get depointed.

I suffocated as she complained that I only listened to one type of music. Then she totally pierced me from within when I saw she would just cavort around the bedroom with any strapping young lad. After a while she didn't even bother hiding the fact that she was more interested in other men. I actually enjoyed it when she started using some of what had by then become my favourite passive-aggressive attacks on them. I couldn't believe some of the low-key, repetitive djentlemen she brought home. I watched, understanding slowly dawning as she tortured them, and why. It was gradual, but we pieced together the remnants of our own war into a gentle, tentative friendship as I saw my now *ex*-girlfriend's psycho moves that were supreme un-churchy evil; that stuff usually blurs 'em.

And it felt like a great way to end the war, on drugs.

THE END